Come Rain or Shine

Come Rain or Shine

101 Devotions for the Journey Home

Brenda Kelley

Pleasant Word
A Division of WINEPRESS PUBLISHING

© 2004 by Brenda Kelley. All rights reserved.

Printed in the United States of America

Packaged by Pleasant Word, a division of WinePress Publishing, PO Box 428, Enumclaw, WA 98022. The views expressed or implied in this work do not necessarily reflect those of Pleasant Word, a division of WinePress Publishing. Ultimate design, content, and editorial accuracy of this work are the responsibilities of the author.

No part of this publication may be reproduced, stored in a retrieval system, or transmitted in any way by any means—electronic, mechanical, photocopy, recording, or otherwise—without the prior permission of the copyright holder, except as provided by USA copyright law.

Unless otherwise noted, all Scriptures are taken from the Holy Bible, New International Version, Copyright © 1973, 1978, 1984 by the International Bible Society. Used by permission of Zondervan Publishing House. The "NIV" and "New International Version" trademarks are registered in the United States Patent and Trademark Office by International Bible Society.

Scripture references marked KJV are taken from the King James Version of the Bible.

Scripture references marked NASB are taken from the New American Standard Bible, © 1960, 1963, 1968, 1971, 1972, 1973, 1975, 1977 by The Lockman Foundation. Used by permission.

ISBN 1-4141-0160-0
Library of Congress Catalog Card Number: 2004103452

[Insert Epigraph]

"The Lord is my shepherd; I shall not be in want. He makes me lie down in green pastures, he leads me beside quiet waters, he restores my soul. He guides me in paths of righteousness for his name's sake. Even though I walk through the valley of the shadow of death, I will fear no evil, for you are with me; your rod and your staff, they comfort me. You prepare a table before me in the presence of my enemies. You anoint my head with oil; my cup overflows. Surely goodness and love will follow me all the days of my life, and I will dwell in the house of the Lord forever."

—Psalm 23

Dedication

For
Thelma Elizabeth Mc Calmon,
my Mother—*my inspiration.*

As I think of my mom, whose life was lived for the Lord, I think of the joy she received from her favorite hymn—"The Old Rugged Cross." As the words of this hymn blessed her in years past, so they still bless us today:

Verse One: "On a hill far away stood an old rugged cross, the emblem of suffering and shame; And I love that old cross, where the dearest and best for a world of lost sinners was slain.

Chorus: So I'll cherish the old rugged cross, till my trophies at last I lay down; I will cling to the old rugged cross, and exchange it some day for a crown.

Verse Two: O that old rugged cross, so despised by the world, has a wondrous attraction for me; for the dear Lamb of God left His glory above, to bear it to dark Calvary.

Verse Three: In the old rugged cross, stained with blood so divine, a wondrous beauty I see; For 'twas on that old cross, Jesus suffered and died to pardon and sanctify me.

Verse Four: To the old rugged cross I will ever be true, its shame and reproach gladly bear; then He'll call me some day to my home far away, where His glory forever I'll share.

Chorus: So, I'll cherish the old rugged cross, till my trophies at last I lay down; I will cling to the old rugged cross, and exchange it some day for a crown."

Table of Contents

Foreword 13

1. Mercy 15
2. "Well, for Pete's Sake . . ." 17
3. "Beam Me Up, Scotty!" 19
4. Keep Those Home Fires Burning! 21
5. Peace 23
6. Anger 25
7. "All Boxed Up and Ready to Go" 27
8. A Mother—Just in Time 29
9. Basking in the Son's Sun 31
10. Beauty and the Beast 33
11. Blue's Clues 35
12. "Burn-o, Burn-o, Efurn-o" 37
13. "But Wait, I Need That!" 39
14. Carrier Pigeons 41
15. Change of Heart 43

16. Check-up 45
17. Comforter 47
18. Crossing Guard 49
19. Crossing the Toll Bridge 51
20. "Don't Turn That Channel!" 53
21. Down Under 55
22. Drainage 57
23. "Extra, Extra, Read All About It!" 59
24. Founding Fathers 61
25. Flash Cards 63
26. Four-Wheel Drive 65
27. Free Delivery 67
28. "Free Shipping and Handling" 69
29. Fresh-Baked Bread 71
30. "Gone Fishing" 73
31. Habitual Habits 75
32. "Hey, Bidder, Bidder . . ." 77
33. Holding Our Promises Eternally 79
34. Humility 81
35. "I Have Half-a-Mind to . . ." 83
36. "I Heard It through the Grapevine." 85
37. "If these Walls Could Talk . . ." 87
38. In the Blink of an Eye 89
39. In the Pink 91
40. "Is That All There Is?" 93
41. "It's Curtains for You!" 95
42. Joy 97
43. Keys 99
44. Kitty Litter 101
45. Love 103
46. Maid Service 105
47. Masterpiece 107

48. Meandering 109
49. Me, Myself, and I 111
50. "On the Side" 113
51. Open House.. 115
52. Pain Reliever... 117
53. "Pop! Goes the Weasel!" 119
54. Pulitzer Prize Winners 121
55. "Put It on My Tab." 123
56. "Putting on the Ritz" 125
57. Quiet Please.. 127
58. "Rags to Riches" 129
59. Red, White, and Blue............................ 131
60. Reflections 133
61. Restoration 135
62. Rock Salt... 137
63. "Selective Hearing"................................ 139
64. "Service with a Smile" 141
65. "Should've Taken the Left Turn at Albuquerque . . ." 143
66. "Sit Still!" 145
67. "Some Days Are Diamonds" 147
68. "Sorry, Wrong Number." 149
69. "Standing Outside the Fire" 151
70. Static Cling...153
71. "Sugar and Spice and Everything Nice" 155
72. "Take Me Out to the Ballgame." 157
73. Tarnished 159
74. The Checkered Flag 161
75. The Eleventh Hour 163
76. The Fruit Bowl 165
77. The "Grim Reaper" 167

78. The Last Supper 169
79. The Pumpkin Patch 171
80. The Root Canal 173
81. "No Time Like the Present" 175
82. "There's Always Room for Jell-O." 177
83. "Time to Weed and Feed" 179
84. "To Each His Own" 181
85. "To Give or Not to Give . . . That Is the Question." 183
86. Trust 185
87. Turnkey Housing 187
88. "Under the Gun" 189
89. Valet Parking 191
90. "Where's the Beef?" 193
91. Whiteout 195
92. "Who Wants to Marry a Millionaire?" 197
93. "X" Marks the Spot 199
94. "Yesterday, When I Was Young" 201
95. "You're in the Army Now!" 203
96. Zigzag 205
97. Grace 207
98. The Price Is Right 209
99. The Lost World 211
100. "Singing in the Rain" 213
101. The Dead of Winter 215

Postlude 217

Foreword

In writing this devotional, my goal is *first* to glorify God and my second is to encourage *you* and help you to personalize your walk with the Lord. As you journey through these daily devotions, I hope you will apply them to your heart and allow the Holy Spirit to minister through them to the need of your life—to give you new understanding—or simply to add a little joy to your day.

My hope is that after you've finished this book your walk with the Lord will be 101 steps closer than when you began!

Blessings,
Brenda Kelley
Vacaville, California

Come Rain or Shine

[Insert Epigraph]

> "For God so loved the world that he gave his one and only son, that whoever believes in him shall not perish but have eternal life. For God did not send his son into the world to condemn the world, but to save the world through him."
> —John 3:16–17

One

Mercy

As I've walked this life's journey I have seen many things. The one thing that will forever remain in my heart is the mercy of the Lord. What is *mercy,* you may ask? Well, the best interpretation I can give is this: When you have done something so horrible you can't even look at yourself in the mirror, and the Lord surrounds you, comforts you, and with a soft voice within tells you he will forgive it all if you ask—*that's mercy!*

Or, let's say someone close to you—one you love more than anyone else, hurts you deeply and walks away with no explanation. You're left sitting there hurting, then hating . . . and then wanting revenge. But suddenly the Holy Spirit comes flooding in and you find your heart melting. The tears flow, and the hurt and hate wash away. *That is mercy!* It's the kind that only God himself is capable of—the kind God can give us to extend toward others when we need to, also. We're blessed to have it at our disposal.

So, whenever you are faced with needing mercy for yourself or extending mercy toward someone else, don't forget to look to the Lord.

"Be kind and compassionate to one another, forgiving each other, just as in Christ God forgave you."
(Ephesians 4:32)

Two

"Well, for Pete's Sake..."

Well, for Pete's sake! My mother-in-law used to say that all the time. It was so cute the way she said it. Either she would mess up on something, or hurt herself, or someone else would do something that got her goat—and out those words would fly. We would often ask her who Pete was. She would just laugh. At any rate, that was mama's line.

Now as I walk my journey with the Lord, that line has whole new meaning for me. For you see, I know who Pete is. Pete represents all of us. When Jesus went to the Cross, He went for Pete's sake, which means He went for *our* sake. So now when I remember that cute little saying of Mama Kelley's, it only reminds me of the love Jesus had for Pete—and for us, too. Thank you, mama, for that!

Come Rain or Shine

"But now a righteousness from God, apart from law, has been made known, to which the Law and the Prophets testify. This righteousness from God comes through faith in Jesus Christ to all who believe. There is no difference, for all have sinned and fall short of the glory of God, and are justified freely by his grace through the redemption that came by Christ Jesus. God presented him as a sacrifice of atonement, through faith in his blood. He did this to demonstrate his justice, because in his forbearance he had left the sins committed beforehand unpunished—he did it to demonstrate his justice at the present time, so as to be just and the one who justifies those who have faith in Jesus."

—Romans 3:21–26

Three

"Beam Me Up, Scotty!"

When I was a young girl living at home my brothers and I would faithfully watch the TV show *Star Trek* every week. I have to say my favorite part of the program was when the officers of the *Starship Enterprise* would find themselves in a pickle on some un-charted planet and would urgently request to be "beamed-up" immediately. And, at the very last second, they were. I would be so relieved!

Now after having a family and finding myself on an *uncharted journey* of my own, you can bet there have been many times I would love to have been beamed-up. But there is only one time the real "beaming-up process" will take place. That is when Christ comes back to earth for those who believe—those who have accepted Jesus Christ as their personal savior. Then and only then will we be *beamed-up* to live on the Father's starship in heaven.

Come Rain or Shine

I wonder if Scotty will be at the helm to beam us up? *Probably not!* Oh well, I guess we can't have everything, can we?

> *"For the Lord himself will come down from heaven, with a loud command, with the voice of the archangel and with the trumpet call of God, and the dead in Christ will rise first. After that, we who are still alive and are left will be caught up together with them in the clouds to meet the Lord in the air."*
> —1 Thessalonians 4:16–17

Four

Keep Those Home Fires Burning!

*J*ust Married is written on the back window of a car I see as I drive down the freeway, reminding me of our early days of my marriage—each of us so in love with the other we would do almost anything to make each other happy. Then, as the years go by, we start to take one another for granted. All too often that "Just Married" sign becomes a "Just Divorced" decree, sometimes handed down by the same judge that married us! We forget to put another log on our fire, and place it on someone else's . . . and soon the "home fires" burn out.

There is another kind of marriage I am involved in. It is my relationship with Jesus. Having this partnership with him helps fill in the gaps in my other marriage. You could say Jesus supplies the logs I need for the "home fire."

Come Rain or Shine

I must also keep in mind that I need to spend intimate, quiet time in prayer with Him, so I do my part in keeping my *spiritual fires* burning, as well. Because one thing is sure, I always want those embers red-hot, and my light shining for Christ.

"Above all, love each other deeply, because love covers over a multitude of sins."
—1 Peter 4:8

Five

Peace

There were times in my life when I thought I would never experience that wonderful thing called *peace*—even when there was nothing outwardly to disturb it.

But there certainly was a lot disturbing it on the *inside*. I sometimes felt like a dingy that had floated out into the midst of a raging sea. And although Jesus was calling my name, I never heard him.

"Why?" You may ask. Well, I was way too busy listening to that storm of the past deep in my soul. Then one day, just when I was sure I would sink, I heard His voice! It was faint, but nonetheless I heard it. And the more I turned my attention to His voice, the clearer it became . . . until it was so clear that the storm inside me was nothing more than a small ripple in the water.

Come Rain or Shine

It was then I learned the secret of obtaining that most precious and priceless gift of peace: it is *focusing on the Lord!* And it's up to us! Do we want the storms of life to take over and rob our peace? Or do we want the loving hand of Jesus to save us and give us a way to enter into a lifelong awareness of true peace? Yes, it is possible—even in the midst of our storms!

"And over all these virtues put on love, which binds them all together in perfect unity. Let the peace of Christ rule in your hearts, since as members of one body you were called to peace. And be thankful."
—Colossians 3:14–15

Six

Anger

How about it? Is anger a word you know a little something about? If we are honest, all of us do. Today a friend of mine made quite an analogy. She told me to put the letter "d" in front of the word anger, and you get "danger." Well, I have to tell you: that statement, in a positive way, hit my spirit like a Mack truck. The Bible tells us we should not sin in our anger, and not give the devil a foothold by holding on to it.

What I glean from this is that when we get angry and don't pray and ask the Lord what we should do next, we fall prey to allowing our minds to be open to a whole host of thoughts and imaginations. The next thing we know, we are caught up in a web designed by Satan that can cause us either to fall into a deep depression, lash out at people around us, throw in the towel, give up, or simply *get an attitude*.

Come Rain or Shine

Whatever the result of letting anger get the best of you, you can bet it turns into *danger*. Anytime we allow an emotion to rule, it creates a new path in our lives that leads us away from the one God has designed for us. Before you know it, there you are out in the middle of a *danger zone* with no spiritual armor and the wolves ready to pounce!

But the good news is, all we have to do is call upon the Lord for help. When we do so, we can rest assured He will come running with stick in hand to ward off the wolves, then turn us around toward the place where we got off course. Sure, anger slowed us down—something Satan loves to do—but as long as we humble ourselves and call upon the Lord, we can get back on course. And the loving *armor of God* we took off can again be placed upon us.

"In your anger do not sin": Do not let the sun go down while you are still angry, and do not give the devil a foothold."
—Ephesians 4:26–27

Seven

"All Boxed Up and Ready to Go"

Sending a package? I sometimes wonder how many packages are sent on a regular business day. Let's just *forget about* Christmas time! I have this picture of UPS, FedEx, and the Postal Service picking up and delivering box after box from Thanksgiving through Christmas. I have to say it is mind-boggling, at the very least, to imagine.

Then I think about being a Christian and being sent out by the leading of the Spirit. It makes me wonder how many of us go out "all boxed up," with no internal freedom, and in turn we spread this bondage to others. Then I wonder how many of us put God in a box, never allowing Him to be all he wants to be in our lives.

Whatever the case, it makes me sad to think of a child of God being boxed in, never having the freedom given to him or her by God himself. Maybe we feel that if we are in a box, or if we *put God in a box,* we can protect ourselves from change, responsibility, and the hurts of this life. Can we seek God for a new freedom today?

"You have not handed me over to the enemy but have set my feet in a spacious place."
—Psalm 31:8

Eight

A Mother—Just in Time

When my mother passed away—too young—I thought I would never get past the pain of losing her. But thankfully God has a special way of healing our hearts. As my life went on I was blessed to marry a wonderful man and to have two beautiful children. Now my children have married and given me four awesome grandchildren.

But something extra special happened between being my a mother and becoming a grandmother. My father met a wonderful woman named Myrle. From the first time we were introduced, I liked her and hoped they would marry.

One day my dad asked me to meet him for breakfast. He said he wanted me to pick out a set of wedding rings for him to give to Myrle. I was so excited that as soon as I left the restaurant I went looking for those rings. I found a set I knew would be perfect. So I purchased them and proudly showed them to my father. As he looked, he realized they were the same set he had bought for my mother a few years before she passed away.

Even though I had seen them, I never made the connection. I felt bad, so I told dad he should return them. But he said to wait and see what Myrle thought. Well, she loved them, and the idea that they were like my mother's made them even more special to her.

What I thought was a big mistake was actually God's way of telling me that Myrle would be a mother who would love me as if she had been there all of my life. Now, that's what I call a mother—*just in time.*

> *"He settles the . . . woman in her home as a happy mother of children."*
> —Psalm 113:9

Nine

Basking in the Son's Sun

Throw on the swimsuit, slather on the lotion, grab a bottle of water, and lay out on your favorite lawn chair. *Ah*—now *this* is the living! Before you know it, you start to get that summer glow. There is only one catch: In order to keep the glow, you have to repeat this process at least once a week. It will be hard but you decide to make time to do it.

Now, let's take a look at "basking in the *Son*." You throw on your clothes, spray on something that smells good, grab your Bible, and sit in your favorite spot at church. You start to think of how wonderful life is walking with the Lord. But there is also a catch to keeping *this* glow—you have to let the Lord lead you every day by listening with all of your heart. So, even though it may be hard at times, what will your decision be today?

Come Rain or Shine

"The Lord is my shepherd, I shall not want. He makes me lie down in green pastures, He leads me beside quiet waters; he restores my soul. He guides me in paths of righteousness for his name's sake. Even though I walk through the valley of the shadow of death, I will fear no evil, for you are with me; your rod and your staff, they comfort me. You prepare a table before me in the presence of my enemies. You anoint my head with oil; my cup overflows. Surely goodness and love will follow me all the days of my life, and I will dwell in the house of the Lord forever."

—Psalm 23

Ten

Beauty and the Beast

If you have children, chances are you have seen this movie at least once if not more times. At the moment my grandson absolutely loves it. I think it's the action he loves best, but it's probably mostly *the beast*.

If by chance you haven't seen it, the storyline is about a prince who fails to allow a little old lady shelter for a night. So she turns into this beautiful princess. After seeing her, he begs her to stay. But it's too late. She turns him into a beast, then leaves a rose under a glass and tells him he has to find someone to love him before the last petal falls. If he doesn't, he will remain a beast forever. The ending is my favorite part. He does find his true love at the very last minute, turns back into his old self, and everything in the castle is restored. *And they live happily every after!*

Come Rain or Shine

In my journey, I hope to always choose beauty over the beast. What I mean is, I want to be obedient to God's Word and direction so that the things I do are things of beauty, not beastly acts.

Also, if you haven't yet, I would encourage you to accept Jesus as your personal Savior before the last petal falls in your life. Then you can become the person God designed you to be—not what the beast (Satan) would deceive you into becoming. I want you to know my discovery that if ever there was true love, it is the Lord's love for us. In the process of letting Him love you, He will restore all that the cankerworm has stolen from your life. And I believe you will live *happily every after.*

"For you created my inmost being; you knit me together in my mother's womb. I praise you because I am fearfully and wonderfully made; your works are wonderful, I know that full well. My frame was not hidden from you when I was made in the secret place. When I was woven together in the depths of the earth, your eyes saw my unformed body. All the days ordained for me were written in your book before one of them came to be."
—Psalm 139:13–16

Eleven

Blue's Clues

~~~

There is a cute children's show that my grandkids love to watch. The name of it is *Blue's Clues*. If you have never seen it, you should try it some time. It is about a dog named *Blue*—a cartoon character, and a guy who is real.

In the show Blue puts her paw print on things that are clues for that particular show. Also, the guy has a notebook, in which he writes down all of the paw print clues.

At the end of the show he figures out the answer to the puzzle of the day from the clues. It is a great learning show for kids.

One day as I was watching with my grandkids, I thought of how Jesus leaves clues all around for *us* to find, so when we need an answer to a question or help in finding direction in a certain situation, it's easier to obtain. But the biggest clue Jesus left is his love for us, shown by his going to the Cross for our sins so that those who accept him as Savior may live eternally in heaven. Let's take the time to look for those clues and to write them in our notebooks . . . so at the end of the day—we will *have a clue!*

"For the Lord gives wisdom, and from his mouth come knowledge and understanding.
—Proverbs 2:6

Twelve

"Burn-o, Burn-o, Efurn-o"

I love to play the game of Monopoly. I remember playing it with my brothers while growing up. When I would roll the dice, one of my brothers would wave his hands over the game board and chant, "Burn-o, burn-o, efurn-o! Make this roll etern-o!" And many times I would roll a bad number. It made me so mad because I believed that his chant had the power to ruin my roll of the dice. Of course as an adult I realize the truth and laugh as I think back on those days.

But I believe many people today buy into the lie of *negative chants* from their childhood. That is one reason why so many walk around defeated. They truly feel that if they try to roll the dice of life they will be a big mistake. I can see how it happens because at one time I believed that lie myself. Of course, I had to let the Lord rescue me by pouring out my heart and soul to him, and in turn He filled me with truth and love.

So now when I roll the dice, or face a risky situation in life that requires faith, all I hear is that the Lord has faith in *me* to overcome it—and the call to trust Him.

"I love you, O Lord, my strength. The Lord is my rock, my fortress, and my deliverer; my God is my rock, in whom I take refuge. He is my shield and the horn of my salvation, my stronghold. I call to the Lord, who is worthy of praise, and I am saved from my enemies."
—Psalm 18:1–3

Thirteen

"But Wait, I Need That!"

It's funny but hearing that statement makes me think about how in the past, when God was trying to rid me of bondage, those exact words would enter my mind. I actually thought I needed to hang on to things that were as bad as poison to me. But that is how bondage works. It starts out subtle, and before long it has attached itself so tightly around you that you truly believe it's been there from *day one*. So, you remain comfortable with it. And all the while it is sucking the life from you—slowly, but surely.

Now that I have allowed God to remove the layers of bondage to "things I thought I needed," I have freedom—more confidence in the person I was created to be—and I am able to love better than ever before. I'll tell you, I would recommend this life-saving process to anyone. Now, instead of telling God I *need* certain things, I remind myself that what I really need is to "let go and let God."

"And my God will meet all your needs according to his glorious riches in Christ Jesus."
—Philippians 4:19

Fourteen

Carrier Pigeons

When I was a child we lived in the country on a couple of acres. We had this large shed we called *the barn*. In this shed my folks had nailed fruit boxes to the wall so that the chickens and pigeons could have a place to nest. I loved to watch as their eggs would hatch and the wobbly babies would come out all wet and ugly. As the weeks passed, I would watch them grow into beautiful birds.

One day a new pigeon joined our family. He flew right to me and let me pick him up. Wrapped around one of his legs was a tiny piece of paper. When I removed it, it was a note to someone. Shortly afterwards he flew away and I never saw him again. I later realized he was a *carrier pigeon* and was trained to return home after delivering his message.

As a child of God I feel like a carrier pigeon. When I first accepted the Lord I was wet behind the ears, wobbly and rather ugly. But as I grow in the Lord, my ears are drying up and my walk is not so wobbly. As I strive to be more like the Lord, I am not so ugly, but rather am becoming beautiful (to the Lord). And now He trusts me to deliver His messages to others, and then fly home to wait on Him for another message that needs delivering. I have to say, "This is the best job in the world!"

"He must hold firmly to the trustworthy message as it has been taught, so that he can encourage others by sound doctrine and refute those who oppose it."

—Titus 1:9

Fifteen

Change of Heart

You have made a decision on something. But you find yourself having a change of heart. For whatever reason, you know it will affect someone or something. It may be for the good, or it may be for the bad. It all depends on the end result.

I know of one change of heart that will always be for the best. That is the decision to accept Jesus as your personal Savior. When you let Jesus change your heart, life will be so much sweeter and definitely more rewarding. Also, you will receive eternal life with Him in heaven. So, if you haven't yet done so, won't you let Jesus give you a *change of heart* today?

Come Rain or Shine

"But thanks be to God that, though you used to be slaves to sin, you wholeheartedly obeyed the form of teaching to which you were entrusted. You have been set free from sin and have become slaves to righteousness."

—Romans 6:17–18

Sixteen

Check-up

As you are going through the mail you come across a little card from your doctor's office reminding you it is time for your medical check-up. So, you call the office and make the appointment. But, after hanging up, you start to worry that you might have something like cancer or high cholesterol. You wonder if it would be better not to go at all. But then, if you do have a problem, ignoring it won't make it disappear. So you go to your appointment. Luckily you get a clean bill of health, and you don't have to think about it again until next year.

Now, let's talk about getting a *spiritual* checkup. You are driving to work when you hear that familiar, still, small voice reminding you it is time to take that Bible study at the church on growing in the

Lord. You begin to worry that if you go to the Bible study there might be more tumors of the past that need uprooting, or a wrong attitude that needs adjusting. But you realize, also, that if you don't go you may become stagnant and stinky. *What's a Christian to do?* I think we all know the answer to that question. Go to the Bible study and let the Lord give you the best spiritual checkup—one available to everyone—and a clean bill of spiritual health.

"Examine yourselves to see whether you are in the faith; test yourselves. Do you not realize that Christ Jesus is in you—unless, of course, you fail the test."
—2 Corinthians 13:5

Seventeen

Comforter

What would you name as your comfort-source? Let's look at some options. Is it food? Is it alcohol? Is it shopping, or something else?

While it is true there are many comforters, there is really only One Who can satisfy our need for comfort and peace of mind. Because, you see, all of the things listed above come with a negative price-tag attached to them. The one True Comforter is the Holy Spirit of God. When we feel like we are falling into a bottomless pit of insecurity, fear, hurt, or jealousy, we can call upon the Name of the Lord, and He will immediately send The Comforter. And if we allow Him, He will begin to cover us in a warm blanket of pure and unconditional comfort. Not only is it free, but it is also a gift we can share with others—one that never runs out. You know . . . like the things in the list do.

Come Rain or Shine

"O, my Comforter in sorrow, my heart is faint within me."
—Jeremiah 8:18

Eighteen

Crossing Guard

～⚘～

We see them everywhere during the school year. They are the ones with yellow vests holding a *stop sign* up as they walk halfway into the crosswalk and summon children to cross the street. I personally appreciate them protecting our kids. What an admirable job they have!

It makes me look at myself in my walk with the Lord. I want to be like a crossing guard for people. What I mean is, I need to remember to protect the people in my life with prayer. I also need to wear my spiritual vest and carry my stop sign so that the enemy *knows* not to mess with me or the people I pray for. My vest is my armor, and my stop sign is the Bible.

Now, if you want to be a crossing guard too, don't forget to pray, to wear your standout vest, and to carry your stop sign at all times.

Come Rain or Shine

"Finally brothers, pray for us that the message of the Lord may spread rapidly and be honored, just as it was with you. And pray that we may be delivered from wicked and evil men, for not everyone has faith. But the Lord is faithful, and he will strengthen and protect you from the evil one."
—2 Thessalonians 3:1–3

Nineteen

Crossing the Toll Bridge

You forgot about that darn toll, so you start digging into your wallet for the two dollars it will take to cross the bridge. *Thankfully* you stopped for coffee and broke your twenty, so you find two ones and pay it with them.

Well, don't we do that in our journey with the Lord? We are going along at a fast pace when, all of a sudden, there it is—the bridge. We forgot all about keeping ourselves prepared to pay the toll. The toll in this journey comes when we have to cross over some barrier we should always be prepared for by being "prayed-up" and "read-up" in God's Word. If not, we may be unable to cross. The best thing to do is keep ourselves broken before the Lord, so that when we need to change, we can. Otherwise, life will take its toll on us!

Come Rain or Shine

"But in your hearts set apart Christ as Lord. Always be prepared to give an answer to everyone who asks you to give the reason for the hope that you have. But do this with gentleness and respect."
—1 Peter 3:15

Twenty

"Don't Turn That Channel!"

As you're flipping through the channels you come upon a movie that you've wanted to see for a long time. So, you pop some popcorn, grab a soda, and sit in your favorite chair to watch it. About thirty minutes into the movie, you realize you have heard seven cuss words and seen two pretty steamy sex scenes.

Deep in your spirit you know you should turn the channel. But your flesh rises up and says, "Don't turn that channel!" So begins the battle. You tell yourself that most of your friends have seen this movie and loved it. They saw nothing out of line. And after all, you *are* watching it in the privacy of your own home. But there's only one hitch; Jesus is aware of everything we watch, as well as everything we do. I'll just bet there is a better movie you can watch if you simply *turn that channel*.

Come Rain or Shine

"The eyes of the Lord are everywhere, keeping watch on the wicked and the good."
—Proverbs 15:3

Twenty-One

Down Under

~~~

*H*ave you ever been *down under*? I haven't, but I have heard that it's nice. Australia is quite a vacation spot for those who like to escape the same old thing. But it is civilized enough for us spoiled ones. I would like to see some of the wildlife there—like Koala bears and the famous kangaroo.

In the Scriptures there is a place referred to as "down under" that I have no desire to visit. It's actual name is "Hell." Oh sure, there are some pretty different creatures there, as well as the devil himself. But I would want to visit *them* about as much as I would like to be bitten by a rattlesnake! I am so thankful that Jesus went to the Cross for me and you. I'll never have to visit that *down under place* as long as eternity lasts.

Come Rain or Shine

"When I saw him, I fell at his feet as though dead. Then he placed his right hand on me and said: 'Do not be afraid. I am the First and the Last. I am the Living One; I was dead, and behold I am alive for ever and ever! And I hold the keys of death and Hades.'"

—Revelation 1:17–20

Twenty-Two

Drainage

Oh no, my sink is clogged and I'm out of Drano®! "Go get the plunger so you can flush the toilet." "The backyard is flooded again; guess the drain is plugged."

What a pain when these things happen! But let me tell you, there is nothing worse than being spiritually "plugged up," because the things that have you stopped up are going to start to stink. And so will everything that comes out of you. They can also make you physically ill.

But *never fear*—there is hope! When you start sensing that your spiritual flow is becoming a trickle, ask the Lord to send down the *heavenly Drano*. Before you know it, you'll be a free-flowing river of spiritual life once again.

Come Rain or Shine

"There is a river whose streams make glad the city of God, the holy place where the Most High dwells."
—Psalm 46:4

Twenty-Three

"Extra, Extra, Read All About It!"

Oh yippee, it's Sunday—the best newspaper day of the week! I must tell you, that *is* exactly how I feel every week. I love the Sunday edition of our newspaper. It has department store ads for the best sales around town, as well as the "home of the week" in the real-estate section. And let's not forget about the comics!

I love it so much that as soon as I wake on Sunday I start thinking about reading it. Right after I put on the coffee I run out to the end of my driveway, without brushing my hair or teeth, to retrieve it. Now, if you knew anything about me, you would know I hate to go outside my door without cleaning up first. So you can see how much the Sunday paper means to me!

Come Rain or Shine

But as wonderful as it is, there is a newspaper out there that has more in it than my cherished Sunday paper. It is God's newspaper, called the *Holy Bible*. It is so thorough it doesn't need to be rewritten each week. It has sales ads—for things like salvation, healing of the body, cleansing of the mind, and freedom of the spirit—that you can't beat, because they are all free! There are sections that will make you laugh, cry, and shout. There is poetry, history, adventure, mystery . . . and more.

So, take my word for it and give God's Word a chance. I'll bet you'll find yourself waking up wanting more, too!

"All scripture is God-breathed and is useful for teaching, rebuking, correcting and training in righteousness, so that the man of God may be thoroughly equipped for every good work."
—2 Timothy 3:16–17

Twenty-Four

Founding Fathers

Thanksgiving has always been a time to be thankful for the ones who came over on the Mayflower. What a long, oftentimes treacherous, journey that finally brought them to their desired destination. Because of their endurance and determination we in America have the awesome blessings with which this country abounds. Thank God for our country's founding founders!

As I make my journey with the Lord I realize more and more how important it is to keep going, even when things become almost too much to bear. I know that I am not only blazing a trail for myself, but for others as well—for my children, my friends, and for even those I may never meet. So, my prayer each day needs to be that I stay on course—no matter how many storms may blow, that I be a trailblazer and a *founder* in my part of the world—for the glory of God, and that I may always be thankful for His provision as I press on.

"Therefore, since we are surrounded by such a great cloud of witnesses, let us throw off everything that hinders and the sin that so easily entangles, and let us run with perseverance the race marked out for us. Let us fix our eyes on Jesus, the author and perfecter of our faith, who for the joy set before him endured the cross, scorning its shame, and sat down at the right hand of the throne of God. Consider him who endured such opposition from sinful men, so that you will not grow weary and lose heart."

—Hebrews 12:1–3

Twenty-Five

Flash Cards

My children loved using flash cards. They would wear me out as I would hold one after another up for them. But even though it was tiresome, I don't regret one minute of helping them learn.

In our journey with the Lord, flash cards are used all the time. As we're faced with a situation, the Holy Spirit will hold up a flash card that will remind us of the right answer to whatever we are facing.

And just as I don't regret helping my children, neither does the Holy Spirit regret helping us.

"So I say, live by the Spirit, and you will not gratify the desires of the sinful nature. For the sinful na-

ture desires what is contrary to the Spirit, and the Spirit what is contrary to the sinful nature. They are in conflict with each other, so that you do not do what you want. But, if you are led by the Spirit, you are not under the law."

—Galatians 5:16–18

Twenty-Six

Four-Wheel Drive

I am now on my second vehicle with four-wheel drive. They are quite convenient to have, especially if you are driving through the Sierras or other mountainous country in the winter. It is nice not to have to stop and put on chains. These vehicles are ready for most any type weather or road condition. Some are even *all-wheel-drive*, which means you don't have to pop it into gear because it changes gears automatically.

My desire is to be like those all-wheel-drive vehicles so that when I come across a rough road or stormy weather, I will automatically shift gears spiritually and *keep on trucking*. Unfortunately, at times I fail and the Lord has to come after me with His tow truck and pull me out. But there's still hope, and I am going to keep trying to have my gears shift-ready. Until they are, I know that I can trust the Lord to help me because He has full-time four-wheel-drive.

"But the Lord is faithful, and he will strengthen and protect you from the evil one."
—2 Thessalonians 3:3

Twenty-Seven

Free Delivery

It's Christmas time again and you have a ton of people to buy for. So, first off you hit the Internet and shop around. As you come across one particular store you see in big bold letters—"Free Delivery." You get excited because that is a store in which you can do most of your shopping. And the best part is you won't have to fight the crowds at the mall or worry that they are sold out of the item you want. Such a deal!

Well, I would like to let you in on another *free delivery*—one that came at Christmastime, too. The best part is you don't have to buy anything to receive it. It is Jesus! He was delivered on Christmas day. He was sent to deliver us from our sins and to reconcile us back to the Father. All you have to do is accept this *free delivery* and your name will be

Come Rain or Shine

written in the *Lamb's Book of Life* for all eternity. Won't you consider this offer today?

By the way—*this* offer is good year round!

"Our Father in heaven, hallowed be your name, your kingdom come, your will be done on earth as it is in heaven. Give us today our daily bread. Forgive us our debts, as we also have forgiven our debtors. And lead us not into temptation, but deliver us from the evil one."
—Matthew 6:9–13

Twenty-Eight

"Free Shipping and Handling"

There you are on the Internet minding your own business when all of a sudden you see something that grabs your full attention. It happens to be an item you have wanted practically all your life. Then you notice it's also forty percent off the regular price. And as if that weren't enough, a flashing sign underneath reads, "Free Shipping and Handling." That's it—you are now *totally sold!* So you pull out the old credit card and purchase away.

Now, let's talk about another item you may not have known you wanted. I guarantee you it is something you need. The item I am describing is *Salvation*. Let me tell you, once it grabs your attention it will never leave your thoughts, and hopefully you will grab for it with all you have. In case you're wondering what it will cost—*it's free!*

By the way, so is the shipping and handling. So why not open up the old ticker and receive away!

"For God did not appoint us to suffer wrath but to receive salvation through our Lord Jesus Christ. He died for us so that, whether we are awake or asleep, we may live together with him."
—1 Thessalonians 5:9–10

Twenty-Nine

Fresh-Baked Bread

Ah—there is nothing like the smell of fresh-baked bread. My mother used to make these yeast rolls that would melt in your mouth. I would eat at least *five* of them with my dinner. To me, that was one of life's greatest pleasures.

It reminds me of the fact that Jesus is the *Bread of Life*. As my mother would teach me about the dear, sweet Savior, I would be intrigued with how much love He had for us. I never wanted my mom to stop talking about it. You see, to me, having a relationship with Jesus truly is life's greatest pleasure.

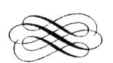

Come Rain or Shine

"Jesus said to them, 'I tell you the truth, unless you eat the flesh of the Son of Man and drink His blood, you have no life in you. Whoever eats my flesh and drinks my blood has eternal life, and I will raise him up at the last day. For my flesh is real food and my blood is real drink. Whoever eats my flesh and drinks my blood remains in me, and I in him. Just as the living Father sent me and I live because of the Father, so the one who feeds on me will live because of me. This is the bread that came down from heaven. Your forefathers ate manna and died, but he who feeds on this bread will live forever.'"
—John 6:53–58

Thirty

"Gone Fishing"

There is a movie by this title about two guys who have fished together for most of their lives. The whole concept of the movie is to show the lengths they will go to go fishing. It turns out they have the worst luck in almost everything they do, including fishing. Of course, it is a comedy so all the stunts they pull are meant to be funny—and they are!

I guess the most important thing that stood out in my mind watching this film is that no matter how many times they failed at catching fish (that is, if they even made it to the lake), they never gave up trying.

When I look at the reason I am here as a follower of Christ, I realize that this is how *I* want to be. I want to make every effort to go fishing for lost souls. And even if, after the many attempts I make, I don't succeed, I never want to stop trying. I want a story written about my life that could be titled—"Gone Fishing."

"As Jesus was walking beside the Sea of Galilee, he saw two brothers; Simon called Peter and his brother Andrew. They were casting a net into the lake, for they were fishermen. 'Come follow me,' Jesus said, 'and I will make you fishers of men.' At once they left their nets and followed him."
—Matthew 4:18–20

Thirty-One

Habitual Habits

Nail biting, overindulging, lying, or giving your opinion without being asked—whatever the bad habit, it can become annoying—even to the one with the habit! On the other hand, there are *good habits*. Things like cleaning up after yourself, paying bills on time, going to church. We all have bad and good habits. But when they become *habitual habits,* even the good ones, can turn sour.

For example, for many the time spent with your family is next to nothing because during the day you work. Then at night you go to every Bible study or meeting there is at church. Eventually your family begins to suffer from lack of attention. Although God loves for us to grow in Him and learn his Word, there must be balance in our lives, as well.

Habitual habits are destructive because they are the ones placed above everything else, and they can become idols. Now of course God must be Number One to us, but sometimes we mistake doing church activities for being with God, and fall prey to other habitual habits that are less-than the best use of time.

Satan is an expert at placing things before you that he knows can easily become habitual habits in your life. Don't let them—or him—fool you.

"If anyone does not provide for his relatives, and especially for his immediate family, he has denied the faith, and is worse than an unbeliever."
—1 Timothy 5:8

Thirty-Two

"Hey, Bidder, Bidder..."

*D*o I hear fifty? *How about a hundred?*

Auctions, they are something else! The few times I have been to one I could barely understand the auctioneer, let alone my living in fear of moving a finger lest he mistake me for a bidder.

But did you know that an auction has already been held for you and me? It was the one where Jesus went to the Cross and gave his life in exchange for ours. Satan tried to outbid him, but there was no way he could. Jesus purchased your life and holds it in trust for you—waiting for you to come to Him. So, if you want to have eternal life, just accept His purchase of it for you at Calvary. It's yours for the taking! And, as a bonus, God has also thrown in the power to overcome fear, confusion, and temptation. What have you got to lose?

Come Rain or Shine

"I have given you authority to trample on snakes and scorpions and to overcome all the power of the enemy; nothing will harm you."
—Luke 10:19

Thirty-Three

Holding Our Promises Eternally

*H*as anyone ever promised you something and you've yet to see it come to pass? Or maybe you made a promise you have not fulfilled. Whichever has occurred, one or both persons can be left feeling hopeless about the promise *ever* coming to pass.

Has God ever given you a promise that hasn't yet happened? Or have you made a promise to Him to do something that you haven't achieved? What I want us to do with both the secular and the spiritual analogy here is to change our perspective from *hopelessness* to *hopeful*.

The way to do this is to realize that humans are going to make promises and not fulfill them. Also, it may not be time for the promise to come to pass, especially when it is a promise from the Lord. You see, when the Lord makes a promise to us, it *definitely* will happen. However, we can prolong the delivery of a good thing by our disobedience. But rest assured, it will arrive, because God's Word is eternal and unchangeable.

"By faith Abraham, even though he was past age—and Sarah herself was barren—was enabled to become a father because he considered him faithful who had made the promise."
—Hebrews 11:11

Thirty-Four

Humility

What are your motives as you set out to live the life God has given you? Or maybe a better question would be, "What are the desires of your heart?"

I ask myself that question many times as I journey, for fear my motives may be *against* the desire God has placed in my spirit. I try to search the God's Word for the correct answers and then apply them as needed.

In Titus, Chapter 3, verses 1 and 2, we're told to, ". . . be ready to do good and to show true humility toward all men." To me this means that in order to truly serve God we must put *others' needs* before our own needs and desires.

Now that sometimes can be way too much for me to do. But thankfully we have a Special Friend in the Holy Spirit, who is always there to forgive us and to show us how to achieve that very important place of true *humility*.

※

"For everyone who exalts himself will be humbled, and he who humbles himself will be exalted."
—Luke 14:11

Thirty-Five

"I Have Half-a-Mind to..."

I have half-a-mind to . . . has been said everywhere from real life to movies. Pertaining to anger, fear, determination, or plain old stubbornness, *sometimes* it is used as a positive, but mostly its use is negative.

As I ponder this frequently used phrase, I can see where it is put into practice way too often, especially in the Christian realm. When we make a commitment to the Lord, we rarely take into account that we need to give our whole mind to Him, not just *half* of it. Believe me, this is more important for us than for the Lord. If we give God only half, Satan will definitely take up the other half, and that will leave us double-minded and unstable.

So the next time you are feeling uncertain in an area, be sure to check in with God and ask Him to show you if you're giving him your whole mind—or just half.

Come Rain or Shine

"Rejoice in the Lord always. I will say it again: Rejoice! Let your gentleness be evident to all. The Lord is near. Do not be anxious about anything, but in everything, by prayer and petition, with thanksgiving, present your requests to God. And the peace of God, which transcends all understanding, will guard your hearts and your minds in Christ Jesus. Finally, brothers, whatever is true, whatever is noble, whatever is right, whatever is pure, whatever is lovely, whatever is admirable—if anything is excellent or praiseworthy—think about such things. Whatever you have learned or received or heard from me, or seen in me—put it into practice. And the God of peace will be with you."

—Philippians 4:4–9

Thirty-Six

"I Heard It through the Grapevine."

Have you ever used that saying when asked how you got certain information? I imagine we all have. What reason did you have for saying it? Was it because you forgot who told you? Or, was it because you didn't feel comfortable giving out the person's name? Or perhaps it was simply a habit . . .

When I stop and think about a grapevine, in my mind's eye I see a lot of twigs wrapped around each other. Kind of a confusing mess! But, and amazingly so, on each twig is the production of some pretty good eating grapes.

It reminds me of how the Bible relates Jesus to being the True Vine and ourselves as being the branches (or twigs). I think of how the *deadness* in us is cut off so that we can bear good spiritual fruit. And no matter how many twisted twigs we grow, at the end of a season God will prune them away and give us a fresh start for the next crop. Where did I get that information, you ask? I guess you could say I heard it from the *true* Grapevine.

"Remain in me, and I will remain in you. No branch can bear fruit by itself; it must remain in the vine. Neither can you bear fruit unless you remain in me."
—John 15:4

Thirty-Seven

"If these Walls Could Talk..."

Ever left the house with a "painted-on" face? I have. It's mostly been over small things, but occasionally there have been some pretty big ones that were upsetting me. Yet we press on. At those times, especially, I'm thankful we have the Lord to talk to and pray things through with.

But there are times you don't get over things so easily. As a child, when this happened I'd usually go to my room and softly talk things out, thinking the only ones listening to me were the walls.

As an adult, I now know those walls weren't listening—but *Jesus was hearing me* loud and clear. And in my childhood, as now, He was always interceding for me.

So, I guess *talking to walls* isn't a waste of time after all.

"Who is he that condemns? Christ Jesus, who died—more than that, who was raised to life—is at the right hand of God and is also interceding for us."

—Romans 8:34

Thirty-Eight

In the Blink of an Eye

~~~

Ever gotten something in your eye? You blink, and there it is to drive you crazy until it comes out. Then, as quickly as it got in there, you blink—and it's gone. At any rate it can be quite annoying.

Or how about when an accident happens "in the blink of an eye?" One minute you are driving along and the next minute a car has rear-ended you. Well, that one doesn't go away as quickly, but it sure did happen fast!

Let me tell you about an experience that *is* going to happen. It is called the Resurrection. This is when Jesus comes back for all believers and takes them home with Him to heaven. Life will be different after that. And it will happen *in the blink of an eye*.

Come Rain or Shine

"Listen, I tell you a mystery: We will not all sleep, but we will all be changed—in a flash, in the twinkling of any eye, at the last trumpet. For the trumpet will sound, the dead will be raised imperishable, and we will be changed."

—1 Corinthians 15: 51–52

Thirty-Nine

In the Pink

As you are waking up you realize a flu bug has bitten you. The timing couldn't be worse! You have just been promoted at work, and today they are having a meeting with *you* as the honored guest. Sound familiar? Well, maybe it is not a job promotion for you, but another event that is important in your life.

So, you head for the medicine chest to find the magic potion to rid you of these sickly symptoms. You start digging until at last there it is— the *perfect* medicine! You take the prescribed dosage and within half-an-hour or so you start to feel better. Then, off to that important event you go!

Have you ever awakened to a mental or heart sickness—knowing you had an equally important day to face? What magic cure is there for that? You realize there is no sense in looking in the medicine cabinet. So, what do you do? Well, let me tell you, there have been many a day I have greeted the day with an "incurable heart illness." But not until I learned that the only cure for it was the healing power of Jesus did I start to get well.

Whether it's a mental or a heart-sickness condition, call out to Jesus, then rest assured that He will come to you with the medicine you need. You can also ask Him to touch you when the illness is physical. Jesus can have you back *in the pink* in no time!

"But for you who revere my name, the son of righteousness will rise with healing in his wings. And you will go out and leap like calves being released from the stall."

—Malachi 4:2

Forty

"Is That All There Is?"

*H*as this question ever entered your mind? It has *mine*; that's for sure. Many times I have looked over situations in my life and pondered the question. That is, up until I realized I was being shortsighted. I was looking at the specific situation and not bothering to look at the *big picture*. You know, like the old saying, "You can't see the forest for the trees."

Well, that fit me to a tee. One day, after many years of wandering through the bevy of trees and not getting anywhere, God came to me and led me by his staff out of the forest and into the land He had prepared for me. And let me tell you, everything I could ever want or need is here. No, it's not that I have arrived. It's quite the opposite. I still have so far to go, but the difference now is that I can see the forest *in spite* of the trees.

Come Rain or Shine

Sure, I still have hard days, but these are nothing like before. Now, after a hard day, instead of asking, "Is that all there is," I can look around and say, "Wow, *look at all there is!*"

"I will walk about in freedom, for I have sought out your precepts."
—Psalm 119:45

Forty-One

"It's Curtains for You!"

*H*as it ever seemed like a black curtain has fallen over your life? Most of us have experienced this happening at one time or another. Whether it came from a boss, a spouse, or a doctor doesn't matter. The truth is that when it comes we are never quite prepared.

I was just at the vulnerable age of fifteen when my mother passed away. I was devastated. Thankfully, I eventually came to understand that time and the Lord *can* heal a broken heart. All these years later, one thing I have learned is that Satan is the one who deceives us into believing that once a tragic thing takes place in our life we can never bounce back. *That is a lie.*

So, the next time tragedy strikes and you feel the curtain fall, call upon the Lord. He will lift the heavy burden and walk you through—into the next step of your journey!

Come Rain or Shine

"Praise be to the Lord, to God our Savior, who daily bears our burdens."

—Psalm 68:19

Forty-Two

Joy

⁂

There is an old church song entitled, "The Joy of the Lord Is Our Strength." Have you ever questioned whether it is possible to experience joy in the middle of a horrific time in your life? Well, *I have*. Maybe if your answer is *yes* to this question, as it was for me, the experience I had may help you have the kind of understanding the Lord gave me.

Back in June of 1999 my husband and I were at church. During worship the Lord gave me a vision of my brother entering heaven. I wondered why He would give me such a vision. The following day I found out. I received a phone call from my brother's oldest daughter, letting me know my brother had died as a result of a crash while riding his motorcycle. As you can imagine I fell apart, thinking to myself, *I never got to say goodbye*. This couldn't have

Come Rain or Shine

been further from the truth, for the Lord reminded me of the vision he'd given me the day before. In that vision I saw my brother turn and look back at me, as if saying goodbye.

Even though I was sad that I would never see my brother here on earth again, I found comfort, and yes, joy, in knowing I would see him again in heaven—where we would never again have to say goodbye. It was at that point that I came to know the true meaning of the words, *"The joy of the Lord is our strength.*

"Go and enjoy choice food and sweet drinks, and send some to those who have nothing prepared. This day is sacred to our Lord. Do not grieve, for the joy of the Lord is your strength."
—Nehemiah 8:10

Forty-Three

Keys

Now *where* are my keys? How many times do you think you've either said or heard that? I bet more times than you'd care to count—if you're anything like me!

Some have tried various things to locate their keys, like the ever-popular "Clapper" gadget, where you clap your hands and a little beeper goes off. Some carry the largest key chain in the world so their keys can't fall down into the sofa cushions. Whatever the effort, those darn keys still somehow get lost. It is almost as though they grew legs and walked off!

But you know, I have knowledge of a set of keys that, once received, can never be lost—or for that matter, stolen. These are called, "the keys to the kingdom." They are the ones that get you into eternity.

Come Rain or Shine

They're the most precious keys you will ever possess. The best part is that they are absolutely *free*. That's because Jesus already paid for them when He went to the Cross and was crucified, then rose again on the third day. It was at that point, when Jesus took hold of those keys knowing He was doing it for us, that we, through him, gained ownership of those keys—and of all eternity!

Through salvation we have the choice either to stay locked up in bondage or use those keys to break out into a new freedom in life that will blow our minds. If we decide to stay locked up, then our spiritual walk will, too. If we decide to use those keys and break free, then spiritually we will be able to touch the lives of people and pass on the "keys of the kingdom," and start helping set others free!

"I will give you the keys of the kingdom of heaven; whatever you bind on earth will be bound in heaven, and whatever you loose on earth will be loosed in heaven."
—Matthew 16:19

Forty-Four

Kitty Litter

You walk in the door and the odor that hits your nose is not one you wanted to breathe in. You realize suddenly that in the two weeks you have been away the kitty litter hasn't been changed. So, you head over to the box and reluctantly clean it. As you are doing this undesirable chore, you begin to understand the importance and blessing of kitty litter. You're thankful you have a fresh bag of it in the garage, too!

What can also be gleaned from this experience is a deeper understanding of the grace and mercy the Lord gives us daily. If we did not have a daily dose of His grace and mercy to cover us, we would be like that soiled kitty litter box. We would stink to high heaven, and chances are no one could stand to be around us—including ourselves. Thankfully the Lord's supply of "kitty litter" never runs out. So don't forget to allow the Lord to extend his grace and mercy to you so that you won't begin to stink!

"But thanks be to God, who always leads us in triumphal procession in Christ and through us spreads everywhere the fragrance of the knowledge of him. For we are to God the aroma of Christ among those who are being saved and those who are perishing. To the one we are the smell of death; to the other, the fragrance of life. And who is equal to such a task? Unlike so many, we do not peddle the word of God for profit. On the contrary, in Christ we speak before God with sincerity, like men sent from God."
—2 Corinthians 2:14–17

Forty-Five

Love

As I sit thinking on the word *love*, I am beginning to realize it is a word that really cannot be explained. It can be given, it can be received, and mostly it can be felt. But truly *explained?* No.

For example, when you find out you and your spouse are expecting a baby and the pregnancy is only four weeks along, what is the biggest feeling you have? Isn't it *love?* Now can you really explain why you are so in love with this new life that is not even one inch in length and you have never seen it? And this life is suddenly someone you would do anything for—even give *your* life?

Well, that is very much like the love God has for us. So much so that He gave His Son to die for us in order to reconcile us back to Himself. Can we explain *that love?* No. But we can surely receive it, feel it, and give it to others.

Come Rain or Shine

"And now these three remain: faith, hope and love. But the greatest of these is love."
—1 Corinthians 13:13

Forty-Six

Maid Service

This house is a mess, you sigh, thinking, "I will never get this place clean. *I need help.*" But your husband is working late and the kids are at school. So, the thought of having a maid enters your mind. Just think, no more sweeping, mopping, or vacuuming. That sounds wonderful! Hmmm, then you could apply your energies to other projects you have been putting off for a long time . . .

You know, come to think of it, that sounds a bit like the idea of our bodies being a house (or temple) to the Lord. Aren't there days when you feel like a total mess inside? Who could ever clean this place up? Well, I have some good news. We have a built-in maid service called the Holy Spirit! He is always ready to clean up any mess or brokenness within us. Isn't *that* wonderful? So, when you feel messy or

Come Rain or Shine

broken, call upon the Lord and he will equip the Holy Spirit with just the cleaning product needed to help make you sparkle again!

"Do you not know that your body is a temple of the Holy Spirit, who is in you, whom you have received from God."
—1 Corinthians 6:19

Forty-Seven

Masterpiece

It seems like every time I go into a department store I end up in the framed art section. I love to look at the different prints and paintings. There are times when one in particular will stand out and grab my attention. It is what I would refer to as a *masterpiece*. I marvel at how a piece of art can quiet all the noise within me and take me to a place of serenity.

This makes me think of when I enter into worship and prayer with the Lord. Just as when I view a great painting, He draws me into His Presence and all the noise fades as I am taken to a place of serenity. It truly takes my breath away! It is here in His Presence I realize, over and over again, that Jesus is the One and only *Master of Peace*.

Come Rain or Shine

"Peace I leave with you; my peace I give you. I do not give to you as the world gives. Do not let your hearts be troubled and do not be afraid."
—John 14:27

Forty-Eight

Meandering

~~~~~~

Have you ever had times when all it seemed like all you did was *meander*? You know, where you walk around not knowing or having a direction in which to go. I am ashamed to say I have had those times way too often in my life.

The reason I am ashamed is that, to me, it means I have squandered valuable time. Even though I realize we should all have a *little* time to meander, it shouldn't become the norm for us.

In my walk with the Lord, too much meandering is especially dangerous. It is during that idle time that Satan will pop up with some pretty interesting temptations. So, I try to ask the Lord for direction every day—then follow His lead.

The next time you find yourself meandering a little too much, try and do what I do: Stop and ask the Lord for directions!

Come Rain or Shine

"If a man is lazy, the rafters sag; if his hands are idle, the house leaks."
—Ecclesiastes 10:18

Forty-Nine

Me, Myself, and I

~~~~~

Are those self-centered words, or what? I certainly have thought that way in my lifetime. Things like—if I do this, what will it benefit me? Or, if I go there, what will be waiting for me? Whatever the event, we will at times wonder what is in it for us. Or, from another side, we are put out because someone isn't thinking the same way we are; therefore *they* must be wrong because I am right.

I would like to look at these words from another perspective. When we start to judge someone for who they are or for what they said, we need to first look at *me, myself and I*. Then, we need to allow the Lord to reveal the "plank" in our eye before we even begin to judge the "speck" in the eye of another. Let's start looking at what we can do for others, and

Come Rain or Shine

I guarantee you that *me, myself and I* will be blessed in the process.

"Do not judge, or you too will be judged. For in the same way you judge others, you will be judged, and with the measure you use, it will be measured to you. Why do you look at the speck of sawdust in your brother's eye and pay no attention to the plank in your own eye? How can you say to your brother, 'Let me take the speck out of your eye,' when all the time there is a plank in your own eye? You hypocrite, first take the plank out of your own eye, and then you will see clearly to remove the speck from your brother's eye."
—Matthew 7:1–5

Fifty

"On the Side"

~~~

*H*ave you ever ordered a meal at a restaurant with those *three little words* attached? I have a few times. But I have a dear friend who orders that way most of the time. I admire that in her because I can see it helps her maintain her perfect weight. There is nothing wrong in ordering your food *on the side*. In fact, I believe we should try it at least every other time we go out.

But when it comes to our walk with God, are we also in the habit of putting Him *on the side*? Do we do it because our subconscious desire is for the excitement of life—or maybe the almighty dollar?

There is nothing wrong with fun or money, but when they become the *main attraction* and God becomes the thing on the side, there lies the problem. We quickly lose balance in our lives. *Why?* Because

Come Rain or Shine

God is so awesome, if He is on the side and other things are front and center, the side is going to flip over and there goes everything to the floor!

We can have many things on the side but we must have only one main course dish, and yes, as you have guessed, that must be the Lord. Then and only then can there be true balance in our lives.

"David and all the Israelites were celebrating with all their might before God, with songs and with harps, lyres, tambourines, cymbals and trumpets."
—1 Chronicles 13:8

Fifty-One

Open House

❦

I remember when my kids were in school and twice a year the teachers would hold an Open House. It was a time to get acquainted with each teacher and also to see the different projects the class was doing.

It was fun sharing this event with my kids. They would take me around explaining each section of the classroom. There was one section for hanging coats and storing lunch boxes, another section for art work, and so on. I could see the joy in the kids' eyes as they shared their world with me. But more than that was the fact that they were, and would always be, my *joy*.

As I recall that time it brings to mind my place with God. I used to be like that, having *open house* only a couple times a year. I would get acquainted

Come Rain or Shine

with God all over again and would show him all the sections of my heart where different things were stored. I could sense the joy God and I both had as I shared my life with Him. Then I realized He knew all about me anyway. He just wanted to have a standing invitation to my *open house*, and also to show me that I was, and always had been, His joy.

"Here I am! I stand at the door and knock. If anyone hears my voice and opens the door, I will come in and eat with him, and he with me."
—Revelation 3:20

Fifty-Two

Pain Reliever

~~~~~

I can't believe it—I burned myself again! That's twice in one week. Sometimes I just want to give up on cooking when this happens. Thank goodness for pain-reliever medicine. If I didn't have that, the pain would make me crazy!

In my journey with the Lord I have been burned a few times, also. Sometimes I cause it, or it happens simply as a result of not watching where I'm going. And, yes, just like getting burned when I cook, I feel like giving up on this journey at those times, as well. But just when I start to feel that way the great pain-reliever (*the Lord!*) comes along, and brings the relief I so desperately need. If it wasn't for that Pain-Reliever, I definitely would be crazy today.

Come Rain or Shine

"He will wipe away every tear from their eyes. There will be no more death or mourning or crying or pain, for the old order of things has passed away."
—Revelation 21:4

Fifty-Three

"Pop! Goes the Weasel!"

Do you remember this familiar childhood song?

> Round and round the mulberry bush the monkey chased the weasel.
>
> The monkey thought that it was in fun. Pop! Goes the weasel!

As far as my spiritual walk goes, I never gave those words much thought. That is, until now. It makes me think how easily we can fall into gossip. You're out with a close friend at the local coffee shop, chatting about this and that. Then someone's name comes up. This someone is a fellow Christian who has recently had some struggles walking their walk. The two of you talk around and around the subject, but all at once—

Come Rain or Shine

Pop! Goes the weasel! And there it is—*gossip*! After an hour passes, you are still gossiping, only now you have "popped off" about three more people.

The time comes for you to head home and something in the pit of your stomach doesn't feel right. You realize what it is. Your weasel has once again *popped!* So here comes the guilt and the depression of knowing you blew it. But never fear, God is there with the forgiveness you need.

Just remember, the next time you are in a conversation and that weasel wants to *pop*, simply breathe a silent prayer for strength to control it. Trust me, I will do the same.

"Search me, O God, and know my heart; test me and know my anxious thoughts. See if there is any offensive way in me, and lead me in the way everlasting."
—Psalm 139:23–24

Fifty-Four

Pulitzer Prize Winners

Are you a wizard at writing—or maybe at music? If so, wouldn't being the recipient of the *Pulitzer Prize* be wonderful? Since its conception, by Joseph Pulitzer, people from all walks of life have vied for that prize. Only a select few have achieved such an honor.

Let's take a look at another prize of honor. It is known as *Salvation*. The wonderful thing about *this* awesome prize is that you don't have to vie for it. Our Creator Himself conceived of it. And people from every walk of life can receive it *free of cost*. The only requirement is to believe that Jesus died on the Cross for you, and to ask Him into your heart and life. If you do this, you will truly be the winner of the most precious prize ever given.

Come Rain or Shine

"Then Jesus declared, 'I am the bread of life. He who comes to me will never go hungry, and he who believes in me will never be thirsty. But as I told you, you have seen me and still you do not believe. All that the Father gives me will come to me, and whoever comes to me I will never drive away. For I have come down from heaven not to do my will but to do the will of him who sent me. And this is the will of him who sent me, that I shall lose none of all that he has given me, but raise them up at the last day. For my Father's will is that everyone who looks to the Son and believes in him shall have eternal life, and I will raise him up at the last day."

—John 6:35–40

Fifty-Five

"Put It on My Tab."

---

*P*ut it on my tab. Now, there's a saying from the past! It makes me think of television shows like *The Waltons* and *Little House on the Prairie*—a time when folks knew one another well enough to trust that payment for goods could, and would, be made in due time. It is heartwarming to know that America was once like that.

Now we have the all-popular "credit card." It's a card that comes with a nice, little *finance charge* attached if not paid in full each month. Even though I use them, it makes me sad that a plastic card has taken the place of human fellowship and kindness. Oh well, that's progress, I guess!

I'll bet if I asked you, most would love to go back to that first system. I can almost bet our heavenly Father would—because He is all about relationship. There's no way to have a meaningful relationship with a piece of plastic. But since it looks like we're stuck with this plastic system, let's keep our *tab* open to fellowship and kindness toward one another—without the finance charge.

"Let us not give up meeting together, as some are in the habit of doing, but let us encourage one another— and all the more as you see the Day approaching."
—Hebrews 10:25

Fifty-Six

"Putting on the Ritz"

Every time I hear that song it makes me smile. I think that's because in my mind I see myself all decked out in the most beautiful evening gown, accessorized with sparkling diamonds, as well as some pretty, cha-cha shoes. Basically, looking better than I have ever looked!

Now I realize looks aren't everything, but being a woman it sure is nice to dress up and feel beautiful from time to time. I really don't think too many women would disagree with that, or men either.

Even though the phrase *Putting on the Ritz* is usually about the outward appearance, there is also a way to *put on the Ritz* on the inside. That is by knowing Jesus as your personal Savior.

Come Rain or Shine

When you accept Jesus into your heart He comes in, cleans out all the garbage, and makes you sparkle like a diamond. Then, He places a song in your heart that causes you to smile the most beautiful smile you have ever smiled—from the inside out.

"Your beauty should not come from outward adornment, such as braided hair and the wearing of gold jewelry and fine clothes. Instead, it should be that of the inner self, the unfading beauty of a gentle and quiet spirit, which is of great worth in God's sight."
—1 Peter 3:3–4

Fifty-Seven

Quiet Please

Libraries—aren't they *wonderful*? When you walk into them it feels as though you've entered a different country. All the hustle and bustle is outside and there is a feeling of peace and solitude inside. But I *have* seen people come in and not experience that quiet peace. As I pondered the reason why some people don't enjoy the atmosphere, I began to see the similarity between the library and spending time in prayer with the Lord.

If we walk into the library expecting a quiet and peaceful atmosphere, we will get it. But if we come into the library with the anxiety of all the things we are trying to accomplish that day, then that is what we will experience. We will see going to the library as one more thing to do, instead of seeing it as a place to have a quiet and peaceful moment or two.

Come Rain or Shine

Now let's compare this to spending time in prayer with the Lord. If we come into his Presence expecting a time of peaceful quietness, then that is what we will experience. But if we see prayer time as just something more on our list of things to do, then that is what spending time with God will be to us.

So, let's start taking advantage of those peaceful, quiet places—and especially of time with God in them. You may be surprised at how much sweeter life can be!

"Then, because so many people were coming and going that they did not even have a chance to eat, he said to them, 'Come with me by yourselves to a quiet place and get some rest.'"
—Mark 6:31

Fifty-Eight

"Rags to Riches"

Have you ever met a self-made millionaire? Maybe you *are* one. I love to hear how they got there, especially the ones that started with next to nothing. Usually they are down to earth and humble when telling their story. I think their attitude comes from the knowledge they obtained on their journey of going from *rags to riches*.

Even though your bank account shows you are not a millionaire, there is a way your heart can show that you are. The first step is to accept Jesus as your personal Savior. Next, allow Him to heal you of the hurts of the past. Then, walk in His love and gifts. If you do this, you will have your very own "rags to riches" story to tell.

Come Rain or Shine

"For you know the grace of our Lord Jesus Christ, that though he was rich, yet for your sakes he became poor, so that you through his poverty might become rich."

—2 Corinthians 8:9

Fifty-Nine

Red, White, and Blue

I was remembering that terrible day—September 11, 2001, and it then crossed my mind how significant our nation's colors are. I thought of *red* being the blood shed by all the people killed or injured, the *white* being the smoke that rose to the sky and the ash that fell to the ground, and the *blue* being the way all who either saw it firsthand or by television felt.

Then I thought of how our nation's colors are significant in the good times. I thought of the red being Christmastime, with loved ones coming together to celebrate the birth of Jesus, white being a wedding gown on a beautiful bride for that most special day, and blue being the oceans that connect us to other nations.

I went further on in thought, looking to my relationship with the Lord. I saw how significant those colors are there, as well. I thought of red as being the blood Jesus shed to cover our sins, white being the pureness and holiness of God, and blue being how the Lord might feel when we reject Him—or when we are hurting.

I guess what I then realized is how perfect and wonderful our nation's colors of *red, white,* and *blue* truly are!

"Cleanse me with hyssop, and I will be clean; wash me, and I will be whiter than snow."
—Psalm 51:9

Sixty

Reflections

I recently purchased a picture for my bedroom. It is of a mallard duck floating on a lake, his reflection gleaming off the water. When I first saw it I felt a spiritual jolt inside. I can only explain that jolt as a way of God reminding me to always check my own reflection to make sure it is revealing His will for my life.

Another thing God showed me in that picture was *peacefulness*. The duck was at peace because his reflection was pure and at rest. That is also something God wants for me.

What a blessing to have that picture hanging in my bedroom, where I can see it every day and be reminded to take the time to let God reflect His purpose and goals for my life!

Come Rain or Shine

"So God created man in His own image, in the image of God he created him; male and female he created them."

—Genesis 1:27

Sixty-One

Restoration

~~~~

I have an oak table in the nook area of my kitchen, and boy does it need restoring. The thought has crossed my mind to get rid of it and buy a new table and chairs. But, for one reason or another, I haven't. Other than the marred top, it is in great shape.

What happens is I sit there thinking what it would take to restore it, and again I put it out of my mind. When we have friends over for dinner it stands out like a sore thumb, so again I begin wanting to restore it.

One day as I was in thought about the table, God spoke to my heart, saying: "You know this table is not much different than people." He explained what He meant. We can see that our heart and life need some restoring, and we start to think about all the work that will go into allowing God to make changes. So, we put it out of our minds until we read our Bible, go to church, or talk with a friend who knows all the little pits in our skin and discolorations in our makeup. And once again we want that restoration process.

From experience I can tell you it is worth all the sanding down, pit repairs, and refinishing process. When God gets done with that part of you, you will not only be surprised at how much better you look, but at how much better you are able to do the things that your journey with the Lord requires.

Oh, by the way, we will all need restoration again from time to time while here on this earth. Just thought I'd warn you!

"And the God of all grace, who called you to his eternal glory in Christ, after you have suffered a little while, will himself restore you and make you strong, firm and steadfast."
—1 Peter 5:10

Sixty-Two

Rock Salt

᯽

Oh, those lazy, hazy, crazy days of summer! One of my favorite things about summer is making and eating homemade ice cream. I love to eat the ice from the ice-cream-maker when some of the rock salt has attached itself to it. For some reason it is more refreshing than eating plain ice. And of course the end results of the rock salt and ice mixture revolving around the outside of the metal container is fabulous ice cream! Whether it's a hand crank or an electric one, I think everyone should own an ice-cream-maker.

Another of my favorite things about summer is getting out more with people and enjoying their company. In doing this I always want to remember to bring along the *rock salt*. So when I'm visiting, people will find my words refreshing and full of flavor. And the end result of our meeting will be a fabulous time—one that has come from the Maker himself.

So, Lord, whether I'm cranky or electrified, please let me share Your *rock salt* with everyone I meet.

"Trust in the Lord forever, for the Lord, the Lord, is the Rock eternal."
—Isaiah 26:4

"Salt is good, but if it loses its saltiness, how can you make it salty again? Have salt in yourselves, and be at peace with each other."
—Mark 9:50

Sixty-Three

"Selective Hearing"

Honey, can you please take out the garbage? No answer. Once again you ask, "Honey, can you please take out the garbage?" No answer. So you reluctantly do it yourself. Half-an-hour later your spouse walks into the kitchen and asks you if you said something. You realize you have been the victim of *selective hearing*.

Do we sometimes have selective hearing with God? I'm sure we all do from time to time. Especially when it comes to getting rid of some garbage in our lives. Then we wonder why God doesn't speak to us more often.

Let's try to keep our ears open to God, as well as to our loved ones, to let them know they are special to us everyday. *Oh*—and don't forget to answer them back!

Come Rain or Shine

"So, as the Holy Spirit says: "Today if you hear his voice, do not harden your hearts as you did in the rebellion, during the time of testing in the desert where your fathers tested and tried me and for forty years and saw what I did."
—Hebrews 3:7–9

Sixty-Four

"Service with a Smile"

Service with a smile! If we look around today we will soon see how *that* motto has become all but obsolete. There are a few places where you can get such treatment, but not as many as there used to be. Maybe it's because of the breakdown of our morals, or that people aren't as happy as they once were. Or could it be because they don't know the true love God has for them?

I know there are days when it takes *all I have* to put a smile on my face—and I even know the love of God! Just think how hard it would be for someone who has never felt that awesome love. So, next time you are out shopping or eating and the person serving you doesn't have a smile, serve them one of yours and let them know God loves them.

Come Rain or Shine

"My command is this: Love each other as I have loved you. Greater love has no one has more love than this, that he lay down his life for his friends. You are my friends if you do what I command."
—John 15:12–14

Sixty-Five
"Should've Taken the Left Turn at Albuquerque..."

Remember when Bugs Bunny would pop up in the middle of a bullring reading a map? He would look around and say: "Hey, this doesn't look right. I guess I should've taken the left turn at Albuquerque." That was one of my favorite cartoons—and is still one of my favorite sayings.

When I think about that cartoon now, it makes me reexamine my spiritual walk. I can remember many times in my life when I was going along full speed, then all of a sudden I pop up and realize I have missed or taken a wrong turn. The worst part is there usually is a mean old bull just waiting to trample me on that detour. So, now I try to listen for the Spirit's still, small reminder to "take the left turn at Albuquerque!"

Come Rain or Shine

"Then the Lord said to Cain, "Why are you angry? Why is your face downcast? If you do what is right, will you not be accepted? But if you do not do what is right, sin is crouching at your door; it desires to have you, but you must master it."

—Genesis 4:6–7

Sixty-Six

"Sit Still!"

Anybody reading this have children? Or been around children? Well, if so, chances are you are familiar with the words, "Sit still." Try as they might, most children find it impossible to do this. *Hmm—sounds a little like being a child of God to me!*

For example, say God gives us a vision of a ministry he is preparing us for. There's only one problem: it won't be taking place for two years. So God says to sit still and wait. The first couple of months aren't so bad. But a year has gone by and you are now getting *pretty impatient*. So, you start to convince yourself you are totally equipped for it—and off you go.

You arrive at step one without a hitch. Next, step two goes pretty well. Then comes step three—and *wham*, the door shuts right in your face. In fact, it feels like your nose is broken. Back you go to the *waiting room*, all the while wondering what happened.

Then, when you get quiet, the Lord speaks to your heart about sitting still and waiting on His timing. As you reach down and pick up the brain you had left behind, you begin to realize the problem was your disobedience to the Lord in *not* sitting still.

Doesn't that sound like something a child of ours, or someone else's, would do? Aren't we glad He is the God of every chance?

"Be still and know that I am God; I will be exalted among the nations. I will be exalted in the earth."
—Psalm 46:10

Sixty-Seven

"Some Days Are Diamonds"

There is a song that goes like this:

> Some days are diamonds, some days are stone.
>
> Sometimes the hard times won't leave me alone.
>
> Sometimes the cold wind blows a chill in my bones.
>
> Some days are diamonds, some days are stone.

I try hard to remember these words so that when a "stone" day comes along I don't totally fall apart. It also helps me remember to pray, especially on the "diamond" days. Because, when we least expect it, the enemy of our souls *will* throw stones our way. Satan knows our weak spots, as well as our weak days. And he lies in wait for the perfect opportunity to attack.

So let us cherish our *diamond days* with prayer and thanksgiving. And let us be prepared for the days of stone by focusing on the one true God, who loves us enough to provide us with a full suit of armor.

"When they kept on questioning him, he straightened up and said to them, "If any one of you is without sin, let him be the first to throw a stone at her."

—John 8:7

Sixty-Eight

"Sorry, Wrong Number."

Isn't it frustrating when you make a call and the person on the other end lets you know you have dialed the *wrong number*? There you are prepared to talk to a certain, special person, and it turns out to be someone else. It's especially frustrating when you're in the middle of a project and they are the only one who knows the next step. In this situation, it really is no big deal because, after all, you *can* simply redial the right number and all is well.

But let's look at a similar situation in our walk with God. We are going along and a temptation comes at us. We need assistance in making the right choice. So, we dial up a friend who is not doing well, and she says, "Go for it! You deserve it." That is what is known as *a wrong number*.

Then we watch a movie about the same temptation we are facing. In the movie the people make

Come Rain or Shine

the wrong choice. Another wrong number! Frustrated and tired, we finally dial up the right number (the Lord!) and ask for help and guidance. He gives it to us. After all, He is the only One who knows what our next step should be.

So, the next time you are faced with a temptation, please make sure your spirit dials the right number first; if not, just say, "Sorry, wrong number!"

"Call to me and I will answer you and tell you great and unsearchable things that you do not know."
—Jeremiah 33:3

Sixty-Nine

"Standing Outside the Fire"

There is a Garth Brooks song entitled, "Standing Outside the Fire." Today I was watching the video to that song. It's about a boy with Down's Syndrome joining the track team at his high school. The video shows him training as his mother drives alongside him in her vehicle. Then it shows him running his first race. Right before the finish line he falls. His dad goes to him and encourages him to finish the race. As he finishes, he raises his arms high and you can see the radiant look of achievement on his face.

It brought me to tears as I thought about my walk with the Lord—how I am often apprehensive about change or meeting a challenge the Lord has set before me. I need to remember that while I'm in training the Lord is right beside me. I need to know that if I fall He will be there to help me back up to finish the race set before me. And when I cross the finish line, I will raise my arms high—and give God all the glory!

"Therefore, since we are receiving a kingdom that cannot be shaken, let us be thankful, and so worship God acceptably with reverence and awe, for our God is a consuming fire."
—Hebrews 12:28–29

Seventy

Static Cling

Laundry day at the old homestead! First you wash, then you dry, then you fold, then you put them away. And all seems right—until it is time to throw the last load into the dryer. You discover you're out of fabric softener sheets!

It might be fine except the last load is the kind of fabric that sticks to your skin when worn if not dried with a fabric softener sheet. Because not only do they soften the clothes, they also prevent *static cling*. Oh, well. Instead of running to the store to get more, you go ahead and dry the clothes without that little sheet.

But, just as you predicted, those clothes stick to your skin like glue when worn. And you spend a week of dealing with static cling when you could have simply gone for more sheets!

Come Rain or Shine

Don't we have a tendency to do that in our walk with God? We start out great, but instead of refilling our hearts and minds with *static cling guard* (praying and reading our Bible), we just keep going until we *run out*. That is when the devil lays temptation, rebellion, or depression on us.

So, why don't we make sure we are stocked up on *static cling guard* every day! Then we can move freely in this world—a world that needs help sorely in the washing and drying cycles of life. *Cling to Jesus!*

"Let us draw near to God with a sincere heart in full assurance of faith, having our hearts sprinkled to cleanse us from a guilty conscience and having our bodies washed with pure water."
—Hebrews 10:22

Seventy-One

"Sugar and Spice and Everything Nice"

I was thinking back on this old saying about little girls that says they're made of: "Sugar and spice and everything nice." An endearing thought. Of course we know in real life even little girls have their moments. I'm sure I drove my parents and five brothers crazy at times.

Even now, as a grown woman, instead of sugar and spice, I occasionally exhibit a dose of sour grapes. *Sorry!* But luckily for those around me on a daily basis, there is hope for those sour days. It is known as prayer. The Bible tells us that *prayer changes things!* It can make bitter better and sour things sweet.

So, the next time you see someone you love having a bad day, please pray for him or her. And if they offend you in any way, forgive. Hopefully they will do the same for you when you need it.

Come Rain or Shine

"Therefore confess your sins to each other and pray for each other so that you may be healed. The prayer of a righteous man is powerful and effective."
—James 5:16

Seventy-Two

"Take Me Out to the Ballgame."

Ever been to a baseball game? Ever wondered what it would be like to be a player? Or are you content being a spectator? I have felt both ways actually. The one thing that ran through my head when I thought about being a player was that I would be crazy to think I could swing a bat, let alone be an asset to the team.

You know, it is probably too late for me to play baseball in the natural sense. But I am glad it is never too late for me, or anyone else, to play *spiritual baseball*. If you don't know the game, I'll try to fill you in. When you are out and about and in conversation with someone and they throw out a need, just swing your bat by praying with them for that need. More than likely you will hit a home run!

Come Rain or Shine

"So neither he who plants nor he who waters is anything, but only God, who makes things grow. The man who plants and the man who waters have one purpose, and each will be rewarded according to his own labor. For we are God's fellow workers; you are God's field, God's building."
—1 Corinthians 3:7–9

Seventy-Three

Tarnished

If you have ever owned fine silver you have learned about tarnish. I really love the look of a silver tea set. Although I have never owned one, I have other things that are made of silver. For instance, I have an ice bucket that, when kept polished, is simply beautiful. When I look at it gleaming I realize that keeping it polished is well worth the effort.

Now, I want to take a look at my heart. Before I accepted the Lord it was covered with tarnish. It looked almost black. Then one day Jesus came along with the best polish and the softest towel ever created—and shined it up. So much so that it looked like a bright, shining light.

But being a Christian doesn't mean it will stay that way on its own. I must daily allow Jesus to polish my heart so that the tarnish doesn't overtake me again. Trust me, it is well worth the effort to present yourself to Him for a "shine."

"What then? Shall we sin because we are not under the law but under grace? By no means! Don't you know that when you offer yourselves to someone to obey him as slaves, you are slaves to the one who you obey—whether you are slaves to sin, which leads to death, or to obedience, which leads to righteousness? But thanks be to God that, though you used to be slaves to sin, you wholeheartedly obeyed the form of teaching to which you were entrusted. You have been set free from sin and have become slaves to righteousness."
—Romans 6:15–18

Seventy-Four

The Checkered Flag

My husband used to race stock cars. When I would go with him the most important part of the race to me was that checkered flag, along with the hope that my husband's car—Number Twenty—would be the first one under it.

There is a race of life being run every day. Every one of us will eventually pass under that checkered flag, and we will either be a winner or a loser. In the spirit realm of Salvation there is no second or third position. We are either saved by believing Jesus is the Savior of the world and accepting him into our hearts—or we aren't. The choice is yours.

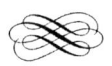

Come Rain or Shine

"Do you not know that in a race all the runners run, but only one gets the prize? Run in such a way as to get the prize."
—1 Corinthians 9:24

Seventy-Five

The Eleventh Hour

&c&

Tomorrow is finals and you have put off studying once again until the last minute. But you think you'll do fine as long as you take the afternoon and cram, cram, cram. Instead, what ends up happening is your brain can only hold so much and starts overflowing. By tomorrow that overflow will be gone. You do wind up passing with a solid *C minus,* but you realize you could have gotten an *A* if you had studied a little each day for two weeks prior to finals.

Even though we are saved by grace, and it is free to everyone, the *eleventh hour* is not really the best time to accept Jesus as your Savior. For one thing, you miss out on walking your journey with Him and miss out on having the sweetest, most intimate relationship you could ever imagine. You know that study time is well worth the effort.

Come Rain or Shine

By the way, overflow on this walk is never lost, for when you are overflowing with the love of the Lord, everyone around you gets a drink of it!

"But the gift is not like the trespass. For if the many died by the trespass of the one man, how much more did God's grace and the gift that came by the grace of the one man, Jesus Christ, overflow to the many!"
—Romans 5:15

Seventy-Six

The Fruit Bowl

On my counter sits my fruit bowl. Just about every week it needs refilling, and the old fruit is thrown out. Off I go to the store and pick out the best fruit I can find, pay for it, and bring it home. My husband, kids, and grandkids appreciate it being around to munch on. It makes me happy to know my efforts are not in vain. The Bible speaks highly of being filled with the fruit of the Spirit and of how *we* can be *spiritual fruit bowls*. The following are the requirements:

First, find out if there are any rotten attitudes or bad feelings you need to let God rid you of. Next, fill up on God's Word and prayer. Then, simply be available to let people take from your spiritual fruit bowl. The fruits of the Spirit are: love, joy, peace, patience, kindness, goodness, faithfulness, gentleness, and self-control.

Come Rain or Shine

"But the fruit of the Spirit is love, joy, peace, patience, kindness, goodness, faithfulness, gentleness, and self-control. Against such things there is no law."

—Galatians 5:22–23

Seventy-Seven

The "Grim Reaper"

You've seen him in movies, and you dread his appearance in your own life. It is scary to think of death and dying. But this— and taxes—are two things we must all face. A lot of people try to act as if dying isn't part of living, when in fact it is probably the biggest part of life itself!

What I mean is, we *should* ask ourselves if we are sure where our spirit is going when our body dies. Did we spend our life on earth getting to know Jesus as our Savior? Or did we spend it getting what we could, no matter what? You see, how we lived our life will determine our life in eternity. So, when you ponder the "Grim Reaper" visiting you, give a little more thought to where your heart is *right now*.

Come Rain or Shine

"Do not be deceived: God cannot be mocked. A man reaps what he sows. The one who sows to please his sinful nature, from that nature will he reap destruction; the one who sows to please the Spirit, from the Spirit will reap eternal life."
—Galatians 6:7–8

Seventy-Eight

The Last Supper

~~~~~

*H*ave you ever gone without food for more than a day—on purpose? In other words, have you tried a scriptural fast? You make a plan to start the next morning, so for dinner you make your favorite meal. As you are eating, you tend to savor every bite as if you will never eat again.

After a good night's sleep morning light breaks through. You wake excited about the results this fast from food will bring. Whether it is to lose weight or because you are in prayer for someone, the end result will make it worth the effort. In any event, it *is* a sacrifice for you.

Whenever I go on a fast from food I try to remember *the Last Supper* Jesus had before going to the Cross. You see Jesus had a plan all along. It was to give His life for a lost and dying world. He too was excited about the results that would come from his sacrifice. The end result was reconciliation for us back to the Father. So even though our fasts, our sacrifices, are not great at all in comparison to the Lord's, we can still give what we are capable of giving, and it's guaranteed to bring worthwhile results.

"When you fast, do not look somber as the hypocrites do, for they disfigure their faces to show men they are fasting. I tell you the truth; they have received their reward in full. But when you fast, put oil on your head and wash your face, so that it will not be obvious to men that you are fasting, but only to your Father, who is unseen; and your Father, who sees what is done in secret will reward you."
—Matthew 6:16–18

Seventy-Nine

The Pumpkin Patch

                  ❦

I enjoy going annually to a local pumpkin patch with my grandkids. I love watching their expressions at the puppet show and seeing their eyes enlarge as they look at the pets in the petting zoo. But most of all I love to watch them pick out their favorite pumpkin. The reason is that each one of them will pick completely different pumpkins. It amazes me how unique each one of my grandchildren is—*not to mention the pumpkins!*

This pumpkin patch adventure is not that different from our relationship with the Lord. I can see where we are the pumpkins, and the Lord is the child picking out the pumpkins. He takes his time as He picks just the right-sized pumpkin for a certain task.

Come Rain or Shine

Sometimes he will need a very small one and sometimes an extra large one. But rest assured, He will find the most perfect one. So don't be discouraged if you are not being picked for a task right now. Be assured, the Lord will have a task that *only you* will be able to do—and be ready when he chooses you to do it.

"For you created my inmost being; you knit me together in my mother's womb. I praise you because I am fearfully and wonderfully made; your works are wonderful. I know that full well."
—Psalm 139:13–14

Eighty

The Root Canal

Several years ago I developed a painful toothache. It became so painful I felt rundown and sick to my stomach. It took over my life until I went to my dentist. From his examination I found that I was in dire need of a root canal. It seems a cavity had traveled up into the root of my back molar, and either I had to have the procedure or lose my tooth. Without hesitation I agreed to the root canal. It was not fun having it done, but after a day or two I felt almost normal. Thankfully that tooth is still intact.

As I think back on that experience, it reminds me of a root canal that the Lord once had to perform on my spirit. He had to reach down and remove a decaying root that was taking over my life—keeping me in a perpetual state of illness. It too was not exactly fun for me—but was extremely necessary. If I had not let the Lord perform the procedure, I believe the malignant feelings would have taken my life.

So, if you are feeling spiritually sick and it's ruining your life, please don't hesitate to go to the Lord and allow him to perform a "root canal" on your spirit—before it's too late and you lose the healthy tissue that surrounds it.

"While Jesus was in one of the towns, a man came along who was covered with leprosy. When he saw Jesus, he fell with his face to the ground and begged him, 'Lord, if you are willing, you can make me clean.' Jesus reached out his hand and touched the man. 'I am willing,' he said, 'Be clean!' And immediately the leprosy left him."
—Luke 5:12–13

Eighty-One

"No Time Like the Present"

*D*on't tell me you are "Mr. or Mrs. Organized"—to the point of being unapproachable and spouting off timetables for others to get things done. Like, if everything is not done perfectly to *your standards*, nobody rests. And heaven forbid it if someone in your circle of family or friends is a wee-bit disorganized!

Don't misunderstand me; there is nothing wrong with keeping things up to par, but when perfectionism becomes your God it becomes a serious problem. *Why?*

If you are a "knit-picker" with the things of the world, you may be a "pick-fuss" in your walk with God, too. This can be deadly when it comes to your being a true witness for Christ to an unbeliever. Your critical comments will most assuredly turn others off. By picking someone's lifestyle apart, you only

Come Rain or Shine

leave them with feelings of rejection, not acceptance and the experience of God's welcoming touch.

A self-righteous attitude is a total misrepresentation of who God is! So, instead of pushing others away by saying, "No time like the present," try saying, "No present like time," and cut yourself some slack today, too!

―――

"But do not forget this one thing, dear friends: With the Lord a day is like a thousand years, and a thousand years are like a day. The Lord is not slow in keeping His promise, as some understand slowness. He is patient with you, not wanting anyone to perish, but everyone to come to repentance."
—2 Peter 3:8–9

Eighty-Two

"There's Always Room for Jell-O."

How many out there love Jell-O®? *I sure do.* Let me tell you, I *always* have room for Jell-O. It is refreshing to eat, the texture satisfies perfectly, and there are so many different flavors to choose from you're bound to love one of them. And talk of versatility! I have seen more recipes than you could shake a stick at. All in all, I think it's great.

As I ponder the greatness of Jell-O, it reminds of the greatness of God. It reminds me I should always have room for God, that reading His Word and praying will refresh me, and that living for Him satisfies perfectly. Like Jell-O, God has so many sides to Him that show us His multi-faceted love. Pursuing a personal relationship with Him, there is no way I will ever be bored, stuffed, or unsatisfied. Make room for Him today!

Come Rain or Shine

"In my Father's house are many rooms; if it were not so, I would have told you. I am going there to prepare a place for you."

—John 14:2

Eighty-Three

"Time to Weed and Feed"

Spring has sprung and with it so have the weeds. It seems as though just last week they were hardly noticeable, but today as you look out into your backyard those weeds are almost as tall as you are! Plus the patch of grass you called a lawn last summer now looks more like a weed garden.

To top it off, the little bit of grass that is still visible is so yellow you wonder if there is *any* hope of saving it. But you decide to go ahead and purchase some weed and feed fertilizer, as well as a weed-eater for those extra motivated growers.

A week after applying the fertilizer to the lawn and weed-eating the giant weeds, you look out into the backyard and smile as you see that the lawn is coming back and the weeds are gone. You feel good knowing your hard work had paid off.

Come Rain or Shine

Well, in our growing seasons with God, we must be careful to weed and feed our spirits, too. Mostly because when the Lord is bringing something forth in us the enemy is close behind to throw weed seed into that new growth. So be quick to grab that weed killer (prayer), and also the feeder (the *Holy Bible*), so that you are well protected against the seeds of the enemy. If you do these things, you will one day look into the mirror and smile, knowing your hard work has paid off.

"A farmer went out to sow his seed. As he was scattering the seed, some fell along the path, and the birds came and ate it up. Some fell on rocky places, where it did not have much soil. It sprang up quickly, because the soil was shallow. But when the sun came up, the plants were scorched, and they withered because they had no root. Other seed fell among thorns, which grew up and choked the plants. Still other seed fell on good soil, where it produced a crop—a hundred, sixty, or thirty times what was sown."

—Matthew 13:3–8

Eighty-Four

"To Each His Own"

To each his own. That statement has flown out of my mouth more times than I can count, usually when I've done something that wasn't too cool. It's easy to use it as a copout, or to avoid being obedient to the Lord.

I've also said it when I've seen a close friend or family member doing or saying something inappropriate. That way I didn't have to take responsibility to urge them to do better.

The next time I'm tempted to say "to each his own," I hope I am wise enough to stop and ask the Lord what He would have me do—*then do it.*

Come Rain or Shine

"When they hurled their insults at him, he did not retaliate; when he suffered, he made no threats. Instead, he entrusted himself to him who judges justly. He himself bore our sins in his body on the tree, so that we might die to sins and live for righteousness; by his wounds you have been healed. For you were like sheep going astray, but now you have returned to the Shepherd and Overseer of your souls."

—I Peter 2:23–25

Eighty-Five

"To Give or Not to Give ... That Is the Question."

So there you are sitting in church minding your own business, when all of a sudden the pastor asks for the "dreaded offering." Ever felt that way? I bet we all have at one point in our lives. Your mind starts to wander through all the bills, the kids' need for clothes, the little extras you want, not to mention *gas for the car*. And here comes that question—"to give or not to give."

I believe God does not want us to be foolish in our giving. But on the other hand, we must ask ourselves if we are foolish in our spending. What it really comes down to is where our heart is. Is it directed to being obedient to God's Word, or is it being directed to compromise?

So, the next time you are faced with that wallet-wringing question, stop and look into the motive of your heart and ask the Lord to give you the *right answer* to the question.

"But just as you excel in everything—in faith, in speech, in knowledge, in complete earnestness and in your love for us—see that you also excel in this grace of giving."
—2 Corinthians 8:7

Eighty-Six

Trust

Trust—where does that word take you? Does it take you to a warm and cozy place, or does it take you to a fearful and lonely place? For me in the past, that word took me to a fearful and lonely place. At the time I had no understanding of what trust was.

Today I find trust to be a warm and cozy place. How did I get there? Through prayer and reading my Bible, God has shown me that when I totally rely on Him (*trust* in him), He'll deal with all that concerns me.

So, the next time you lack the courage or strength to step out into your journey, just call on the Lord and He will be there to help.

Come Rain or Shine

"*Some trust in chariots and some in horses, but we trust in the name of the Lord our God.*"
—Psalm 20:7

Eighty-Seven

Turnkey Housing

    Now if you want to buy a house with everything, *turnkey housing* is for you. If you don't quite understand what *that* is, I'll explain. *Turnkey housing* is where a person purchases a home with everything from furniture to silverware included. Basically, all the buyer has to bring along is clothing. Now granted, you will have to leave your old furnishings behind, but what awaits you will most likely be worth it.

    There is also another kind of turnkey housing that is from the Lord Jesus Christ. His Word promises that if you will accept Him as your personal Savior, He will enter into your heart and make everything brand-spanking-new. And the best thing about this is—it is free of charge! Though you will have to leave some things behind, it will *definitely* be worth it. Because what the Lord will furnish you with will be worth living for and precious as fine diamonds.

"Yet to all who received him, to those who believed in his name, he gave the right to become children of God—children born not of natural descent, nor of human decision or a husband's will, but born of God."
—John 1:12–13

Eighty-Eight

"Under the Gun"

Time is flying by and you have only three out of twenty things finished. Do you start to feel a little pressured? Or, maybe you have only ten minutes to pick up your six-year-old from school, and the traffic is horrible. Or, here's an all-time favorite: you are expecting your paycheck to be a certain amount, and it comes up four hundred dollars short because the person doing payroll made a mistake. You have already sent off the payments for your bills, and you know *one* of them is going to bounce. How do you handle this *under the gun* business anyway?

There were times when I didn't handle it too well. And then there have been a few times when I felt as though I handled it much better. What was the difference in my being able to handle or not handle *under the gun* situations?

Come Rain or Shine

I have noticed that when things start falling in on me, if I stop and pray for peace and wisdom I can handle the pressure way better than if I try to take it on myself. Because it seems that every time I ask God for help, He sends it. And usually the help He sends is simple. I learn it is my call to either get stressed out or to just relax and do my best.

It's like my mom used to say; "You can't squeeze blood out of a turnip." In other words, you can only do what you can do. So, the next time you feel pressured, just call on the Lord for help and He will confiscate that *gun* you feel under and remind you—you're only a turnip! He's the Gardener.

"Consider it pure joy, my brothers, whenever you face trials of many kinds, because you know that the testing of your faith develops perseverance."
—James 1:2–3

Eighty-Nine

Valet Parking

~~~~~

All of the big hotels have it, as well as all of the fancier restaurants. It is such a *wonderful* luxury, I think. You drive to your destination and someone opens the door of your car and helps you with your luggage (if checking into a hotel), then, if needed, helps with your coat. As you head to your destination, they whisk your car off to park it in a safe parking area. *Ah*—how nice to have such treatment!

But there is one little catch; and it's called the *valet-stub*. This is needed to retrieve your car when you're ready for it. What happens if you lose that precious little stub? Well, first you have to show your license to the head honcho of valet parking. Then, once you prove you really are who you say you are, then comes their hunt for your keys, which can be hard—especially so if there are more than a hundred valet parked cars. But generally you eventually get your car back.

After your car is returned you remember the tip, which you double because you lost the stub and they had to work harder than usual. That is what goes with the territory of luxury on this earth. There is always a catch.

Now just think, there is a place that all children of God will be some day—a place that will have every luxury imaginable. There will be *no catches* and *no fees*. It is called *Heaven,* and from what I understand it is going to be awesome. I don't know about you, but I sure am looking forward to pulling up to the pearly gates and having Jesus waiting to open the door and lead me into His "no catch" eternal life of luxury.

"Do not store up for yourselves treasures on earth, where moth and rust destroy, and where thieves break in and steal. But store up for yourselves treasures in heaven, where moth and rust do not destroy, and where thieves do no break in and steal. For where your treasure is, there your heart will be also."

—Matthew 6:19–21

Ninety

"Where's the Beef?"

There was a popular commercial that aired a few years ago in which a little old lady asked this question. I think it was about her ordering a hamburger with little meat on it.

As I was thinking about this advertisement, the Lord reminded me of something that happened a couple of months ago. I was going to get my Bible to read and I heard the Lord speak to my heart and say, "*Ah, baby wants its milk.*" Well, it caught me by surprise, and I asked the Lord what that statement meant. So, He began revealing to me that my growth in Him would always be stunted if I didn't start eating the meat of God's Word. In other words—stop being a baby and grow up!

Sounds a wee bit harsh, doesn't it? Yet these were the best words I could have heard. Because I felt just like a "right of passage" had come my way, and believe me I didn't realize I was ready to graduate!

If God had not shown me the truth about myself, I would still be using the Bible as a way to remain a person who would need constant and repetitive care, not a person who could reach out and help others in their quest for spiritual maturity. You see, God was saying the same thing to me that the little old lady was saying to that person running the hamburger joint—*"Where's the beef?"*

"Anyone who lives on milk, being still an infant, is not acquainted with the teaching about righteousness. But solid food is for the mature, who by constant use have trained themselves to distinguish good from evil."
—Hebrews 5:13–14

Ninety-One

Whiteout

~~~~

I can almost guarantee that every office has a bottle of this stuff tucked away somewhere for those little mistakes made on paper. I have to admit that I have a bottle myself and have had to use it more than once. It really is a nice thing to have on hand. How it works is, if you are writing or typing something and afterwards see that you made a mistake—*whiteout®* comes into play. All you do is brush a little on, let it dry, and it instantly covers the error. So instead of throwing the paper away and starting over, you can write or type the word correctly over the whiteout.

You know, walking with the Lord is like having your own personal bottle of whiteout. Because when Jesus went to the Cross He shed his Blood to *cover* our sins. When we sin, we can ask for His forgiveness, and the Blood of Christ does for our souls something much like the whiteout does for the paper: It corrects the mistake we made so we can start over, right where we left off, without having to throw out everything we have accomplished for the Lord. It lets us go on right from there.

"But if we walk in the light, as he is in the light, we have fellowship with one another, and the blood of Jesus, his Son, purifies us all from sin."
—1 John 1:7

Ninety-Two

"Who Wants to Marry a Millionaire?"

I saw this show last year about a group of women vying for the chance to marry a man who was a millionaire. It was sad to watch women who had never met this man parade themselves around wearing everything from satin evening gowns to bikinis, in hopes of being the best-looking one of the bunch.

Call me old-fashioned, but I like to get to know a man before I marry him! Sure enough, at the end of the show a beautiful damsel is chosen, and they are married then and there. Now *isn't* that romantic!

Well, as most of us can guess, that wedded bliss lasted all of two weeks. I think just long enough for the honeymoon to take place. As I watched this show unfold, I thought of how different the show was from my wedded bliss with Jesus. You see when I asked him into my heart, I didn't have to parade around to prove my worth to him. He already knew me. Jesus had gone to the Cross and had given all He had for me—*His life*. The reason He did was so I could spend eternity with him. Now that is worth way more than a million dollars!

As far as the honeymoon goes, all I can say is, "It isn't over yet!"

"Jesus replied: 'Love the Lord your God with all your heart and with all your soul and with all your mind.'"
—Matthew 22:37

Ninety-Three

"X" Marks the Spot

*E*ver watch one of those old treasure-hunting movies? You know, the movies with pirates and ships that travel from one island to another, because they found a map that promises them a buried treasure that will make them richer than their wildest dreams? And of course the most important mark on the map was the infamous X. I call it infamous because the characters would do anything to find the treasure that was behind that X—even kill for it!

It makes me think of life today, of how people are following these maps and mowing others down in hopes of getting to the *hidden treasure* first. This desperate way of living has even infected Christians. Not that Christians are better than anyone else—but we should know better.

Come Rain or Shine

We should realize that there is only *one* Treasure, and there is more than enough of it to go around.

That treasure is Jesus. He is to be shared, not hoarded! He brings renewal, not destruction. Yes, He has the map and He is the X that marks the spot. So, let us become pirates for Jesus and sail our ships island to island to share this Treasure with everyone we meet!

"My purpose is that they may be encouraged in heart and united in love, so that they may have the full riches of complete understanding, in order that they may know the mystery of God; namely, Christ, in whom are hidden all the treasures of wisdom and knowledge."
—Colossians 2:2–3

Ninety-Four

"Yesterday, When I Was Young"

Ah—sweet days of youth! How wonderful it was to jump and run without hurting something. How wonderful to eat all the food you wanted, without thinking about calories or carbs. I guess we all long for those days from time to time. But the older I get, the more I understand the value of living *in the moment*.

Maybe that's why our bodies slow down as we age. This slowing-down-process has taken me from being a Martha to being a Mary. It has taught me to look outside myself and toward the destiny God has called me to. And to not take things for granted. I'm not saying everything I did in the past was wrong. In fact, a lot of it was right. What I am saying is that the slowing-down-process has taught me to *allow change to come*, because only then can you stop living off the events of yesterday.

Come Rain or Shine

So, allow the slowing-down-process of your life to come, and then embrace the changes as you would a newborn baby.

"No one sews a patch of unshrunk cloth on an old garment, for the patch will pull away from the garment, making the tear worse. Neither do men pour new wine into old wineskins. If they do, the skins will burst, the wine will run out and the wineskins will be ruined. No, they pour new wine into the new wineskins, and both are preserved."
—Matthew 9:16–17

Ninety-Five

"You're in the Army Now!"

*W*ell, you have done it—*you're in the Army now!* You have gone through all the paperwork, completed boot camp, received your uniform, and are stationed three thousand miles away from home. Even though it was the hardest thing you ever accomplished, you are still happy with your decision. Now your journey to become the best soldier you can be is well on its way.

When I accepted Jesus as my Savior, I knew that in order to grow in the Lord I needed to read my Bible faithfully, pray regularly, attend church each week, and be willing to go wherever God would send me. Even though it wasn't always easy, and at times I failed miserably, I am still glad I made the choice to join "His army." Though I have gone through many trials and rewards on this journey, I know I have only just begun to become the best "soldier-for-Christ" I can be.

"Endure hardship with us like a good soldier of Christ Jesus. No one serving as a soldier gets involved in civilian affairs—he wants to please his commanding officer."
—2 Timothy 2:3–4

Ninety-Six

Zigzag

My mother used to make a lot of my clothes when I was a child. I loved it when she would border them with "zigzag." She would make several rows, and each row would be a different color.

My mother has passed away, but whenever I see an article of clothing with a zigzag design on it, I smile as I lovingly think about her making my clothes with my favorite pattern sewn on their edges. *Thanks, Mom!*

Today mom's zigzag pattern has taken on a deeper meaning for me. God showed me that like the zigzag pattern of my childhood, perfectly finishing off an article of clothing, so His gifts sewn into the fabric of our lives do the work of perfecting us. *Thanks, God!*

Come Rain or Shine

"*Do not conform any longer to the pattern of this world, but be transformed by the renewing of your mind. Then you will be able to test and approve what God's will is—his good, pleasing, and perfect will.*"

—Romans 12:2

Ninety-Seven

Grace

~❦~

About two years ago I went to a tea/birthday party that a mother was giving for her daughter. It was lovely . . . and fun, as we all dressed in our finest clothes and adorned ourselves with hats and gloves to match. But the one thing that stayed with me is the graciousness extended to each person by the mother and the person hired to put on the tea.

Each lady got to choose a teacup and also the type of tea she wanted, as well as to dine on some pretty amazing goodies. I felt *undeserving* of this gracious treatment and, honestly, was a little uncomfortable, to say the least.

In the past two years since that lovely tea, the Lord has spoken to my heart about *grace*. It is true we don't deserve the grace of God, but that is what makes it so wonderfully special. Like at the lovely tea party, God invites all of his children to join in, pick their favorite cup, and drink all the *spiritual tea* they want. The Father has everything we need. All we have to do in the Sweet Name of *Grace* is receive.

"But where sin increased, grace increased all the more."
—Romans 5:20

Ninety-Eight

The Price Is Right

Come on down, you're the next contestant on *The Price Is Right!*

I think those words are the most exciting part of the show. I love to watch that person jump up out of their seat and run down the aisle to the podium awaiting them. Then the next challenge is being the one who comes closest to the price of the item up for bid, without going over. Once that happens they get to play a game to win anything from a dining room set to a new car.

And last, but certainly not least, is the *Showcase Showdown*— which is the ultimate in prizes! This is where two players bid on a showcase, and whoever comes closest to the actual price without going over, wins. There are a lot of wonderful prizes in those showcases.

Come Rain or Shine

But I would like to tell you about another *Price Is Right* concept. The wonderful thing about this one is that there is no level you must achieve, and all can have the Showcase Showdown, as well. The only requirement is to accept Jesus Christ as your personal Savior—the One who paid the *ultimate price* on Calvary so we might have the Prize that God has set before us.

I pray that when the Lord calls *your* name you will not hesitate to, "*Come on Down!*"

"As Jesus was walking beside the Sea of Galilee, he saw two brothers, Simon called Peter and his brother Andrew. They were casting a net into the lake, for they were fishermen. 'Come, follow me,' Jesus said, 'and I will make you fishers of men.' At once they left their nets and followed him."
—Matthew 4:18–20

Ninety-Nine

The Lost World

The movie came out in the '90s. It is about a dinosaur park that was created by taking ostrich eggs and injecting them with dinosaur DNA—*and out hatched baby dinosaurs!* Yet this experiment failed, because you just can't keep those darn creatures caged up.

But the brain behind this park decided he wanted to try it again, and *lo and behold* it failed again. So it is labeled, "The Lost World," because if anyone tries to enter the island, they most likely will lose their life to these wild, supposedly extinct, creatures.

After watching this movie I can see a correlation between creating, caging, and controlling these dinosaurs and controlling the sin of this world. Just like the dinosaur, sin cannot be caged up and controlled by man, meaning we can't tuck it away somewhere and then visit it without it taking over—and costing us our lives.

The only way to overcome sin is to have faith that Christ died on the Cross to destroy sin. Then ask Him into your heart, and for forgiveness. Then, and only then, can sin be put to death. So, have you taken in Christ's DNA and found out the truth about your own sin in *this Lost World?*

"When you were dead in your sins and in the uncircumcision of your sinful nature, God made you alive with Christ. He forgave us all our sins, having cancelled the written code, with its regulations, that was against us and that stood opposed to us; he took it away, nailing it to the cross. And having disarmed the powers and authorities, he made a public spectacle of them, triumphing over them by the cross."
—Colossians 2:13–15

One Hundred

"Singing in the Rain"

I'm singing in the rain, singing in the rain . . . .

Gene Kelly sure knew how to get your toes a-tapping and wake up your desire to get out in the rain and splash up a storm. Normally just the thought of going out when it's raining is inconvenient, to say the least.

I wonder if this is how most Christians feel when the Lord wants to rain down his Spirit upon us. Possibly the inconvenience alone is enough to not want it. Believe me, I have felt that way more than once in my walk with the Lord. But thankfully, there have been one or two Gene Kelly's that crossed my path and gave me a desire to get out in the rain and splash God's love onto others who need to be watered.

Come Rain or Shine

"On the last and greatest day of the Feast, Jesus stood and said in a loud voice, 'If anyone is thirsty, let him come to me and drink. Whoever believes in me, as the scripture has said, streams of living water will flow from within him.'"
—John 7:37–38

One Hundred-One

The Dead of Winter

Here it is—January, and almost every plant in your yard is looking pretty dead or sickly. As you take inventory, fear sets in that some of them might not make it to spring. So, you take every precaution possible to prevent the wintry elements from taking a toll on your beloved foliage.

I wonder if you've ever been in what felt like the *dead of winter* in your walk with the Lord? *I have.* I felt as though there was no way I was going to make it to spring. I recall the fear that gripped my heart almost daily. It would take a toll on my body and I would literally feel ill. But, thankfully, the Lord would send someone to me or remind me that all I needed to do was take precious precautions—like reading God's Word, praying, and trusting. He would never leave me nor forsake me because I am one of the beloved plantings in His garden of life. And actually, so are you!

"The Spirit of the Sovereign Lord is on me, because the Lord has anointed me to preach good news to the poor. He has sent me to bind up the brokenhearted, to proclaim freedom for the captives and release from darkness for the prisoners, to proclaim the year of the Lord's favor and the day of vengeance of our God, to comfort all who mourn, and provide for those who grieve in Zion—to bestow on them a crown of beauty instead of ashes, the oil of gladness instead of mourning, and a garment of praise instead of a spirit of despair. They will be called oaks of righteousness, a planting of the Lord for the display of his splendor."

—Isaiah 61:1–3

Postlude

Dear Reader,

As you conclude this book, my hope is that *come rain or come shine* you will realize that the Lord has created a special journey just for you—and that He is with you on it every step of the way!

Blessings and best wishes,
Brenda Kelley

To order additional copies of

Come Rain or Shine

Have your credit card ready and call:

1-877-421-READ (7323)

or please visit our web site at
www.pleasantword.com

Also available at:
www.amazon.com
and
www.barnesandnoble.com

Printed in the United States
30265LVS00001B/121-213